Best Rail Trails
WISCONSIN

Help Us Keep This Guide Up to Date

Every effort has been made by the author and editors to make this guide as accurate and useful as possible. However, many things can change after a guide is published—hiking trails are rerouted, establishments close, phone numbers change, facilities come under new management, and so on.

We would love to hear from you concerning your experiences with this guide and how you feel it could be improved and kept up to date. While we may not be able to respond to all comments and suggestions, we'll take them to heart and we'll also make certain to share them with the author. Please send your comments and suggestions to the following address:

The Globe Pequot Press
Reader Response/Editorial Department
P.O. Box 480
Guilford, CT 06437

Or you may e-mail us at:

editorial@GlobePequot.com

Thanks for your input, and happy trails!

Best Rail Trails
WISCONSIN

MORE THAN 50 RAIL TRAILS THROUGHOUT THE STATE

PHIL VAN VALKENBERG

REVISED BY KEVIN REVOLINSKI

FALCONGUIDES ®

GUILFORD, CONNECTICUT
HELENA, MONTANA
AN IMPRINT OF THE GLOBE PEQUOT PRESS

TO MY FAMILY,
WHO ALWAYS MOTIVATED ME TO DO MY BEST

FALCONGUIDES®

To buy books in quantity for corporate use
or incentives, call **(800) 962–0973**
or e-mail **premiums@GlobePequot.com**.

Project Manager: David Legere
Text design: Sheryl P. Kober
Layout Artist: Maggie Peterson
Maps: Trailhead Graphics, Inc./Sue Murray, copyright © Morris Book Publishing, LLC
Map research materials courtesy of DeLorme Atlas and Gazetteer™
Photos by Phil Van Valkenberg unless credited otherwise.

Library of Congress Cataloging-in-Publication Data

Van Valkenberg, Phil, 1945-
  Best rail trails Wisconsin : more than 50 rail trails throughout the state / Phil van
Valkenberg; revised by Kevin Revolinski.
    p. cm.
  ISBN 978-0-7627-4676-7
  1. Rail-trails—Wisconsin—Guidebooks. 2. Outdoor recreation—Wisconsin-—Guidebooks.
3. Wisconsin—Guidebooks. I. Title.
  GV191.42.W6V35 2009
  917.75--dc22
                        2008033805

Printed in the United States of America
10 9 8 7 6 5 4 3 2 1

CONTENTS

INTRODUCTION

Our pace is so fast. In the ever changing and evolving world of technology, we literally cannot keep up with the times. Once upon a time the train seemed like the epitome of the modern world. Sleek and bold trains were our nation's pride and joy and symbolized the possibilities of a world beyond the one in which we lived. Connecting large cities and small towns, used for transportation and for the shipping of goods, the train was the pulse of the nation.

But times change. With the advent of the car and the building of mass highways, trains became a secondary form of transportation. And dreams die. Railroad tracks were abandoned. Nature took over, and where once a track split through the woods, only a ghost of the track remained.

Enter the Rails-to-Trails Conservancy (RTC), a group of outdoor enthusiasts who in 1986 began the arduous task of transforming abandoned railroad tracks into nature trails. Banding together with other conservation groups, RTC removed tracks and molded the trails into wonderful paths running through urban and rural areas.

Children often take their first bike trip on a rail trail.

There is something remarkable about traveling the nation in pursuit of the abandoned railroad track now converted to greenways, bicycle paths, and nature trails. What better way to see the country than by traversing these rail beds?

A Little Wisconsin Rail History

Outdoor recreation and access to the beauty of nature are top priorities for millions of Americans in the new millennium. Lifestyles include stressful occupations and many time demands. The need for the calming and physical health that recreating in the great outdoors can provide has become increasingly important. The development of rail trails is a big part of the effort to fulfill those needs.

Wisconsin got an early start with rail trails. Shortly after the Chicago and Northwestern Railroad abandoned its line from Elroy to Sparta in 1965, the state bought land with the goal of creating a recreational trail. Renewed interest in self-propelled outdoor activities like hiking and bicycling prompted them to try an entirely new type of facility in a beautiful part of the state that previously had very little in the way of attractions. The Elroy-Sparta State Trail was an immediate hit and remains the state's most popular destination trail today.

The birth of the state of Wisconsin coincided with the development of the railroad as a viable transportation technology. Before the railroad, people and goods traveled by watercraft or wagon. Lake Michigan, Lake Superior, the Mississippi River and the Fox-Wisconsin Waterway were the connections to and from a spiderweb of primitive roads. Canals, which had been important in states just east of Wisconsin, were proposed here, but all major projects failed thanks to the coming of the railroads.

The key to railroad superiority was its ability to function in any weather. Rivers and lakes froze over in winter. Wagon trails, bad anytime of year, became impassable with winter snow and ice and springtime mud. In 1836, two years before statehood, a rail line between Milwaukee Harbor and the Mississippi was proposed and was completed in the mid-1850s.

There were no doubts about the benefit of the railroad to the state's booming economy. At midcentury Wisconsin produced half the nation's lead and was number two in wheat production. Land values tripled and quadrupled along railroad rights-of-way. River and steamboat lines were abandoned. Towns went wild trying to outbid each other in luring the railroads with bond issues and other subsidies. In the meantime, the railroads were locked in bitter competition with each other. At times they built parallel tracks through the same regions and ignored equally profitable areas in their efforts to annihilate their rivals.

By 1900 the expansion of railroad trackage had stopped. Railcar loading peaked in 1927, when thirteen railroad companies served the state.

In the waning days of rail passenger service, railroads staged one of history's great competitions, vying for patronage with luxury and speed. Classic streamliners like the Burlington Zephyr, the "400," and the Hiawatha raced between Chicago and Minneapolis at speeds in excess of 100 miles an hour.

Despite tough competition from trucking and from automobile and air travel, the railroads show no signs of disappearing. Today, high-speed passenger rail seems to be an innovative transportation solution for the future. Freight rail is doing very well. What shook out from the lean railroad years is a legacy of abandoned rail lines. Outdoor recreation seekers are the beneficiaries.

The History of the Rails-to-Trails Conservancy

The beauty of RTC is that by converting railroad rights-of-way for public use, it has not only preserved a part of our nation's history but also allowed a variety of outdoor enthusiasts to enjoy the paths and trails.

Bicyclists, in-line skaters, nature lovers, hikers, equestrians, and paddlers can enjoy the trails, as can railroad history buffs. Many of Wisconsin's rail trails are wheelchair accessible. Throughout Wisconsin there are sixty active RTC trails, and each year more are added. You can find trails near cities and rural trails far from the madding crowd. In many ways we have come full circle. By preserving part of our history, we can enjoy the trails as if time stood still.

The concept of preserving these valuable corridors and converting them into multiuse public trails began in the Midwest, where railroad abandonments were most widespread. Once the tracks came out, people started using the corridors for walking and hiking while exploring railroad relics ranging from train stations and mills to bridges and tunnels.

Bike trailers are a common sight on rail trails.

Although many people agreed with the great new concept, the reality of actually converting abandoned railroad corridors into public trails was a much greater challenge. From the late 1960s until the early 1980s, many rail trail efforts failed as corridors were lost to development, sold to the highest bidder, or broken into pieces.

In 1983 Congress enacted an amendment to the National Trails System Act directing the Interstate Commerce Commission to allow about-to-be-abandoned railroad lines to be "railbanked," or set aside for future transportation use while being used as trails in the interim. In essence, this law preempts rail corridor abandonment, keeping the corridors intact for trail use and any possible future use.

This powerful new piece of legislation made it easier for agencies and organizations to acquire rail corridors for trails, but many projects still failed because of short deadlines, lack of information, and local opposition to trails.

The Rails-to-Trails Conservancy was formed in 1986 to provide a national voice for the creation of rail trails. RTC quickly developed a strategy to preserve the largest amount of rail corridor in the shortest period of time: a national advocacy program to defend the new railbanking law in the courts and in Congress, coupled with a direct project-assistance program to help public agencies and local rail trail groups overcome the challenges of converting a rail into a trail.

The strategy is working. In 1986 the Rails-to-Trails Conservancy knew of only seventy-five rail trails and ninety projects in the works. Today there are more than 1,000 rail trails, and many additional projects are under way. The RTC vision of creating an interconnected network of trails across the country is becoming a reality.

The thriving rails-to-trails movement has created more than 7,700 miles of public trails for a wide range of users. At present, Wisconsin has more than 1,300 miles of rail trails, a number ranking among the top state totals in the nation, and the count's not over by any means. New trails come on-line each year as rights-of-way are acquired and developed. Today it is possible to cover 110 miles of nearly continuous rail trail from the center of the state to the Mississippi. In urban areas, rail trails are becoming important commuter links allowing people to leave the car in the driveway and bike or walk to work or school. The Wisconsin Department of Natural Resources has been a statewide and nationwide leader in trail development and will continue to be so in the future. Through its efforts, a cross-state route from Milwaukee to the Mississippi will one day be a reality.

Benefits of Rail Trails

Rail trails offer safe, scenic, easily accessible recreation. Grades on rail trails are gentle, rarely topping 3 percent even in the state's southwestern hill country. That makes them great for kids, casual bicyclists and hikers, and people with disabilities. Often the grades double as snowmobile or cross-country ski trails in the winter.

In urban areas rail trails act as linear greenways through developed areas, efficiently providing much-needed recreation space while serving as utilitarian transportation corridors. They link neighborhoods and workplaces and connect congested areas to open spaces. In many cities and suburbs, rail trails are used for commuting to work, school, and shopping.

In rural areas rail trails can provide a significant stimulus to local businesses. People who use trails often spend money on food, beverages, camping, hotels, bed-and-breakfasts, bicycle rentals, souvenirs, and other items. Studies have shown that trail users have generated as much as $1.25 million annually for a town through which a trail passes.

Rail trails have allowed many communities to recapture their heritage by revitalizing depots and historic structures, such as bridges, tunnels, mills, factories, and canals. These structures shelter an important piece of history and enhance the trail experience.

Wildlife enthusiasts can enjoy the rail trails, which are home to birds, plants, wetlands, and small and large mammals. Many rail trails serve as plant and animal conservation corridors, and, in some cases, endangered species can be found in habitats located along the route.

Recreation, transportation, historic preservation, economic revitalization, open-space conservation, and wildlife preservation—these are just some of the many benefits of rail trails and the reasons why people love them.

The hard hats check each other out.

The strongest argument for the rails-to-trails movement, however, is ultimately about the human spirit. It's about the dedication of individuals who have a dream and follow that vision so that other people can enjoy the fruits of their labor.

How to Get Involved

If you really enjoy rail trails, there are opportunities to join the movement to save abandoned rail corridors and to create more trails. Donating even a small amount of your time can help get more trails up and going. Here are some ways you can help the effort:

- Write a letter to your city, county, or state elected official in favor of pro-trail legislation. You can also write a letter to the editor of your local newspaper highlighting a trail or trail project.

- Attend a public hearing to voice support for a local trail.

- Volunteer to plant flowers or trees along an existing trail or spend several hours helping a cleanup crew on a nearby rail trail project.

- Lead a hike along an abandoned corridor with your friends or a community group.

- Become an active member of a trail effort in your area. Many groups host trail events, undertake fund-raising campaigns, publish brochures and newsletters, and carry out other activities to promote a trail or project. Virtually all of these efforts are completed by volunteers, and they are always looking for another helping hand.

Whatever your time allows, get involved. The success of a community's rail trail depends upon the level of citizen participation.

How to Use Rail Trails

By design, rail trails accommodate a variety of trail users. While this is generally one of the many benefits of rail trails, it also can lead to occasional conflicts among trail users. Everyone should take responsibility to ensure trail safety by following a few simple trail etiquette guidelines.

One of the most basic etiquette rules is "Wheels yield to heels." The figure below indicates the correct protocol for yielding right-of-way. Bicyclists (and in-line skaters) yield to other users; pedestrians yield to equestrians.

Generally, this means that you need to warn users (to whom you are yielding) of your presence. If, as a bicyclist, you fail to warn a walker that you are about to pass, the walker could step in front of you, causing an accident that could have been prevented. Similarly, it is best to slow down and warn an equestrian of your presence. A horse can be startled by a bicycle, so make verbal contact with the rider and be sure it is safe to pass.

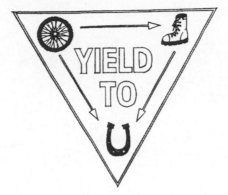

Here are some other guidelines you should follow to promote trail safety:

- Obey all trail rules posted at trailheads.

- Stay to the right except when passing.

- Pass slower traffic on the left; yield to oncoming traffic when passing.

- Give a clear warning signal when passing.

- Always look ahead and behind when passing.

- Travel at a responsible speed.

- Keep pets on a leash.

- Do not trespass on private property.

- Move off the trail surface when stopped to allow others to pass.

- Yield to other trail users when entering and crossing the trail.

- Do not disturb the wildlife.

- Do not swim in areas not designated for swimming.

- Watch out for traffic when crossing the street.

- Obey all traffic signals.

How to Use This Book

At the beginning of the book, you will find a map showing the location of Wisconsin's rail trails. Before the text description of every trail, we provide the following information:

- **Name:** The official name of the rail trail.

- **Activities:** A list of icons tells you what kinds of activities are appropriate for each trail.

- **Location:** The end points of the trail.

- **Length:** The length of the trail, including how many miles are currently open.

- **Surface:** The materials that make up the rail trail vary from trail to trail. This heading describes each trail's surface. Materials range from asphalt and crushed stone to the significantly more rugged original railroad ballast.

- **Wheelchair access:** Some of the rail trails are wheelchair accessible. This allows physically challenged individuals the opportunity to explore the rail trails with family and friends.

- **Precautions:** Adverse trail conditions, street crossings, and other potential difficulties are included here, as well as any trail fees or park rules you should be aware of before beginning the trail.

- **Food and facilities:** Here we will indicate the towns and areas near the rail trails in which restaurants and fast-food shops are available. If a restroom is available near the trail, the book will provide you with its location. Parks, playgrounds, and swimming areas are also included.

- **Seasons:** Most of Wisconsin's trails are open year-round.

- **Access and parking:** The book will provide you with locations where you can park to access the rail trails.

- **Rentals:** Some of the rail trails have bicycle shops and skating stores nearby. This will help you with bike or skate rental information. If you are having problems with your equipment, you can have it checked out at the store.

- **Contact:** The names and phone numbers of chambers of commerce, tourism bureaus, state agencies, or similar organizations are listed here. The selected contacts can provide additional information about the trail and its condition.

- **Map:** The main rail trails and state park trails featured in this book include basic maps for your convenience. It's recommended, however, that street maps, topographic maps such as USGS quads or DeLorme's *Wisconsin Atlas and Gazeteer,* or a state atlas be used to supplement the maps in this book.

- **Mile-by-mile description:** The major rail trails featured will have a mile-by-mile description, allowing you the chance to anticipate the experience of the trail.

KEY TO ACTIVITIES ICONS

 ATVs

 Bird-watching

 Camping

 Cross-country Skiing

 Dog Walking

 Fishing

 Horseback Riding

 In-line Skating

 Mountain Biking

 Road Bicycling

 Snowmobiling

 Snowshoeing

 Swimming

 Walking/Day Hiking

 Wildlife Viewing

KEY TO MAP ICONS

P Parking

I Information

 Restrooms

R Rentals

 Camping

Picnic Area

Food

Note: All map scales are approximate.

Rail Trails
WISCONSIN

Wisconsin
Top Rail Trails

Wisconsin's
Top Rail Trails

1 AHNAPEE STATE TRAIL

The Ahnapee State Trail connects two fascinating maritime towns, Sturgeon Bay and Algoma, and provides access to Potowatomi State Park and the many attractions of Door County.

Activities:

Location: Sturgeon Bay to Casco

Length: 39.3 miles of rail trail, plus 2.8 miles of town trail and on-street routes in Sturgeon Bay and 0.8 mile of city trail and on-street routes in Algoma

Surface: Crushed limestone with wood-planked bridges; some asphalt and concrete sections on the Sturgeon Bay city trail

Wheelchair access: Yes

Precautions: The town trails in Sturgeon Bay are not fully developed all the way to Sawyer Park; public streets must be used. Through the Stoney Creek Swamp, between Sturgeon Bay and Maplewood, the rail bed is elevated above the marsh level by a foot or more, which makes straying from the trail a wet experience. Horseback riders use the same trail bed as other users. Wisconsin State Trails have a carry-in/carry-out policy. Make provisions for carrying out any refuse. The trail between Algoma and Casco is mostly open, with occasional shaded stretches. The use of sunblock is advised. No fees are required on this state trail, but donations are gladly accepted at trailside boxes. In winter you must have a Wisconsin snowmobile registration or nonresident trail use sticker.

Food and facilities: Numerous restaurants and fast-food places are found in Sturgeon Bay and Algoma. A tavern/restaurant and a convenience store are in Forestville. Taverns are in Maplewood and Rio Creek. A cafe, a couple of taverns serving food, and a gas station convenience store are in Casco. Water and flush toilets are at Sawyer Park in Sturgeon Bay and Legion Park in Forestville. Flush toilets, water, and a playground are at Cherry Blossom Park on the city trail in Sturgeon Bay. Pit toilets are just north of County Road M near Algoma and at Forestville Dam Park. Playgrounds are at Forestville Dam Park and at Legion Park.

Seasons: Open year-round

Access and parking: From Wisconsin Highway 42/57 in Sturgeon Bay, take Green Bay Road northeast for 0.7 mile to Maple Street. Turn right (east) and go 1 block to Sawyer Park. For equestrians or hikers, from WI 42/57 in Sturgeon Bay, take Shiloh Road (look for brown and white trail signs) south for 1.0 mile to a T intersection with Leeward Street and turn right (west). After 0.2 mile turn left (south) on South Neenah Avenue and go 0.3 mile to the Ahnapee State Trail parking lot on the left. From WI 42 in Algoma, take Navarino Street west for one-half block and then turn right (north) into the Ahnapee Trail parking lot. Park on-street on Wisconsin Highway 54 in Casco.

Rentals: Ahnapee Trails Campground, Algoma, (920) 487–3707

Contact: Algoma Area Chamber of Commerce, (800) 498–4888 or (920) 487–2041, www.algoma.org. Door County Chamber of Commerce, (800) 53–RELAX or (920) 743–4456, www.doorcountyvacations.com. Friends of the Ahnapee, (920) 388–0444.

|||||||||||||||||||||||||||||||||||||||||||||||||||||||||||||||||||||||||||||||||||||

Your Ahnapee State Trail adventure will be a mix of the beauty of the land and the mystery of the lake. Rich traditions of sailing, fishing, and shipbuilding contrast with quiet rural farming lifestyles. You can always count on fresh fish on restaurant menus in Sturgeon Bay and Algoma, and there is a lot more than trail travel to enjoy on the Door Peninsula.

The trail was once the route of the Ahnapee & Western Railroad. Trains served the countryside by hauling the bounty of the land—lumber and farm products—to the lake ports. Today the rail bed opens up the peninsula's inland to recreation seekers.

If you are bicycling, you may choose to start in Sturgeon Bay at Sawyer Park on the town's waterfront. The scene hardly seems midwestern. Next to the park is the U.S. Coast Guard station, where the cutter *Mobile*

The harbor view is fascinating in Sturgeon Bay.

Bay is often docked. Across the canal you'll see the Palmer Johnson yard where luxury yachts and racing boats are handcrafted. Beyond the iron lift bridge, large lake freighters are docked at Bay Shipbuilding, the only yard on the Great Lakes big enough to handle 1,000-foot-long ships.

There's more than scenery in Sturgeon Bay. Near Palmer Johnson is the Bayou on Third Street Restaurant, where they add a Creole touch to traditional Great Lakes whitefish.

Potowatomi State Park, just north of Sturgeon Bay, is a wonderful place to visit. Sitting on a limestone bluff overlooking the bay, the park is blessed with a beautiful forest of white paper birch, maple, and pine trees. An observation tower at the north end of the park offers a grand overview of the bay and the city. From the Ahnapee State Trail you can reach the park on a bicycle via city streets.

Riding southwest, you must follow city streets for the first 0.4 mile. Begin by going south on South Neenah Avenue for 3 blocks. Turn right (west) on Redwood Street and continue for 1 block. Turn left (south) on Madison Avenue, which becomes Green Bay Road, and follow it for 0.2 mile to the intersection of Lansing Avenue, where the city portion of the Ahnapee Trail begins (look for a brown and white sign on the south side of Green Bay Road). The trail is asphalt here and runs past Bay Mall, a possible alternate starting point if you want to avoid riding busy Green Bay Road.

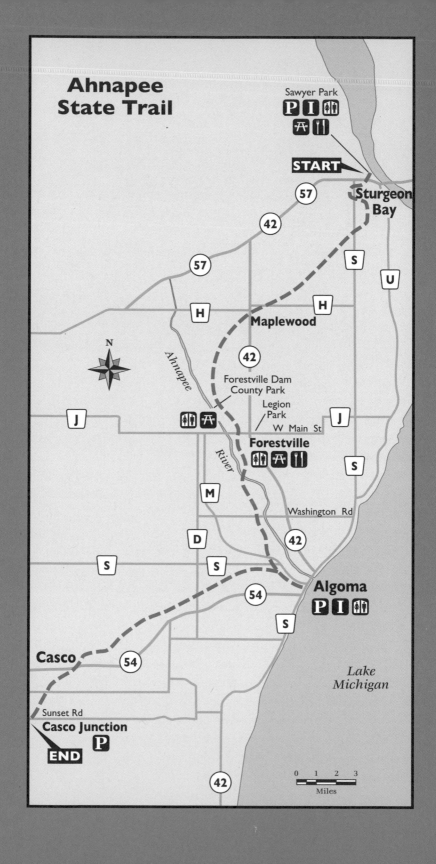

Ahnapee State Trail

Sawyer Park

START

Sturgeon Bay

57

42

57

H

S

U

H

Maplewood

Ahnapee

42

Forestville Dam County Park

N

Legion Park

J

J

W Main St

Forestville

River

S

M

Washington Rd

D

42

S

S

54

Algoma

S

Casco

54

Lake Michigan

Sunset Rd

Casco Junction

P

END

42

0 1 2 3
Miles

Past Bay Mall the trail becomes a wide concrete sidewalk that underpasses WI 42/57 and puts you out at a cul-de-sac on residential Hudson Avenue. Follow Hudson Avenue south for 2 blocks to a dead end and turn left (east) on the crushed stone Ahnapee Trail. This trail portion will zigzag to the east and south, passing Cherry Blossom Park on the way, for 1.1 miles until it reaches the Ahnapee State Trail parking lot on South Neenah Avenue. This parking lot is the best starting point for hikers and equestrians.

The first few miles of trail cover nearly flat terrain through a mix of farm-land and woodlots. At 3.0 miles (from the Ahnapee State Trail parking lot) you cross the Stoney Creek Swamp. The swamp is on both sides of the trail bed, which is elevated about a foot above the water level. A mix of cattails and tamarack trees fills the swamp. At 6.4 miles you reach the crossroads village of Maplewood, distinguished only by a grain elevator and a tavern.

From Maplewood the trail makes a sweeping turn to the southeast to parallel the course of the Ahnapee River. At 10.9 miles you reach Forest-ville Dam County Park, where you can let children enjoy the playground. Another 0.3 mile farther the trail crosses County Road J, which is West Main Street in the pleasant town of Forestville. Turn east on County Road J and go 0.3 mile to Forestville's downtown. One block north on North Grand Avenue is Legion Park, a nice resting spot with a modern playground.

Along the first 0.8 mile south from Forestville Dam County Park, you'll have close encounters with the Ahnapee River, which meanders to the edge of the trail in several places. Another river view comes at 13.3 miles, when you cross the Ahnapee on a special bridge constructed for the trail. All of the original railroad bridges were removed before the state took possession of the right-of-way.

South of the bridge the trail passes through an interesting natural area. On the west side you'll hear a steady chorus of croaking frogs in the spring and early summer. The marshy land to the east of the trail is a hatch-ing area for turtles, which sometimes bore holes in the trail. Aspen trees, white paper birch trees, and grapevines line much of the trail.

At 17.3 miles you reach the junction of the Algoma/Sturgeon Bay link and the Algoma/Casco link. A trail section paralleling Perry Street (County Road S) now takes you east from the junction another 0.8 mile, nearly all the way downtown. From there you can go 1 block south on Sixth Street and east one-half block on Navarino Street to the trailhead parking lot. At this point you are just one building west of WI 42, which is Fourth Street. Fourth

Street becomes Lake Street to the south; it leads to the business district several blocks away, where you'll find an ice-cream shop and a bakery.

Algoma is a contrast to Sturgeon Bay. If you continue riding east from Fourth Street for 0.3 mile on Navarino Street, you'll come to the breakwater with the Algoma Pierhead Lighthouse at the end. The rugged concrete barrier seems to hold back the power of Lake Michigan. An elevated walkway to the light gives some idea of how rough the weather can get. Pleasure boats line the harbor, which is actually the outlet of the Ahnapee River. The breakwater is usually populated by anglers trying their luck. Check out the no-nonsense commercial fishing boat, the *La Fond,* tied up at a dock along the harbor channel.

Along Navarino Street you'll pass Netto Palazzo, a unique flatiron building at the corner of Fourth Street and Navarino Street. It houses a variety of shops, an espresso bar, a deli, and, of all things, the Motorcycles of Italy Museum. Across the street is Hudson's Restaurant, which serves fresh fish and chowder in a dining room overlooking the harbor. Farther east is the Von Stiehl Winery, located in a beautiful nineteenth-century brick building. Guided winery tours are conducted every day from May though October; sampling is encouraged. On the north side of the harbor channel bridge on Fourth Street is the Captain's Table restaurant, where fresh fish is the specialty.

Another contrast on this tour is the Algoma to Casco trail link. The surrounding terrain is more rolling and almost entirely agricultural. The trail has some sheltering trees and brush growth, but is much more open than along the Sturgeon Bay to Algoma stretch. The payoff on the way to Casco is the bounty of wildflowers that flourish along the sunny trail sides. There are no services along the 9.6 miles between the trail junction in Algoma and Casco. Taverns in Rankin and Rio Creek can be accessed with short side trips on County Roads D and K, respectively. Plans are in the works to put in toilets and a parking lot in Casco.

The little village of Casco is a typical Wisconsin farm town with a couple of taverns, a, cafe, and a convenience store. The trail continues another 2.4 miles southwest of Casco to an abrupt end at Sunset Road in Casco Junction. The meeting of the rail lines was the only reason it was ever put on a map. Future trail extensions will run the route all the way east to the lake port of Kewaunee.

Door Peninsula's Waters Are a Ship Graveyard

The Door Peninsula is Wisconsin's gateway to the world. From Native American canoes to three-masted schooners to giant thousand-foot lake freighters and luxurious pleasure boats, the surrounding waters of Green Bay and Lake Michigan have long been paths of commerce and pleasure. The sight of a vessel on the horizon kindles feelings of excitement, anticipation, and admiration for the grace found in all sailing ships. Tragically, not all ships make it to port.

In 1680 the French adventurer René-Robert Cavelier de La Salle sailed to the peninsula on the *Griffin*, the first European sailing ship to ply the Great Lakes. He traded with the Native Americans and loaded the ship with furs to send back to Montreal. The ship's bounty was to pay for a western expedition to find wealth or perhaps a passage to China. La Salle waved the ship's crew farewell and set off overland with his exploring party. The journey would bring him fame as the discoverer of the outlet of the Mississippi River. The *Griffin* was never seen again.

The *Griffin* was just the first of hundreds to fall prey to the treacherous waters around the peninsula. The name Door comes from the name the French gave it: Porte des Morts, Death's Door. Wrecks from the age of sail and the age of steam lie in its depths, preserved by the cold, dark waters. The sunken ships are protected as underwater archaeological sites by the Wisconsin State Historical Society. You can learn about some of the wrecks on the Society's Web site at www.seagrant.wisc.edu/shipwrecks. You can also find insights into the peninsula's nautical traditions at the Door County Maritime Museum on the waterfront between the Coast Guard station and iron lift bridge in Sturgeon Bay.

2   BADGER STATE TRAIL

Follow part of the line where the glaciers stopped at the end of the last ice age and ride through a quarter-mile tunnel on this newest rail trail, which connect Madison to Illnois and its trail system.

Activities:

Location: South of Madison to Illinois state border

Length: 34.1 miles (to be expanded to 41 miles when it connects to Capital City State Trail and Southwest Path in Madison)

Surface: Crushed limestone with wood-planked bridges; the future section from Madison to Paoli will be asphalt.

Wheelchair access: Yes

Precautions: Sun Valley Parkway heading east from Paoli does not offer trail access though it may appear so on maps. Some bikers and hikers may choose to follow Wisconsin Highway 69 south from Paoli 1.2 miles to Henry Road and the town of Basco to pick up the trail. The highway, however, is quite busy. Though many do this already, it is not recommended for children because of frequent road crossings. The trail's landmark tunnel requires use of a flashlight, and if you're on a bike it would be better to walk it here. The 12-mile stretch between Monticello and Monroe offers no facilities. Wisconsin State Trails have a carry-in/carry-out policy. Make provisions for carrying out any refuse. No trash receptacles are provided on-trail. The Wisconsin State Trail Pass is required for bicyclists age sixteen and older ($4.00 daily or $20.00 annually). The trail pass also covers usage such as cross-country skiing, horseback riding, and bicycling on state mountain bike trails and other rail trails. Passes can be purchased at the New Glarus Depot, New Glarus Woods State Park, at many local businesses, and at self-pay stations at trail-access parking lots. In winter you must have a Wisconsin snowmobile registration or nonresident trail use sticker.

Food and facilities: There are restaurants and bars in Paoli, Belleville, Monticello, and Monroe, but they are located off the trail. Monticello has a swimming pool and playground. The Monticello trail parking lot has pit toilets, and there are restrooms at the public library in Belleville right behind the trail parking lot. These are available during library hours. Twining Park in Monroe offers restrooms, water, and a playground.

Seasons: Open year-round

Access and parking: To start at the north end, you can park in Paoli and take County Road PB 1.1 miles north to Purcell Road and then go east 1.7 miles to pick up the trail. There is no parking lot here. Others might opt to take County Road PB 0.2 mile south from Paoli to WI 69 and follow it 1 mile to Henry Road. The trail is 0.2 mile east of here. The trail shares a parking lot with the Sugar River State Trail in Monticello. Go east on Lake Avenue (Wisconsin Highway 39) and go south on County Road F to where it curves east and becomes County Road EE. This may be WI 39 on older maps. The lot is on the north side of the road before you reach the trail.

Rentals: New Glarus Depot, New Glarus, (608) 527–2334. In Madison: Williamson Street Bike Works, (608) 255–5292, www.willybikes.com. Machinery Row Bicycles, (608) 442–5974, www.machineryrowbicycles.com. Yellow Jersey, (608) 257–4737, www.yellowjersey.org.

Contact: Badger State Trail (New Glarus Woods), (608) 527–2334. Green County Trails Information Line, (608) 527–2910. Monroe Chamber of Commerce, (608) 325–7648.

|||||||||||||||||||||||||||||||||||||||||||||||||||||||||||||||||||||||||||||||||||||

The Badger State Trail runs the dividing line between the glaciated region and unglaciated "driftless" zone of southern Wisconsin. Thus the scenery is quite beautiful, ranging from rocky hills to rolling farmland. Part of the Ice Age Trail follows the same route. The Badger Trail was a long time coming: Plans had been in the works since 1976 to convert this rail bed, which runs from Madison south all the way to the Illinois state line. In July of 2007 the southern portion was officially opened. Once complete it will connect to the Capital City and Military Ridge State Trails. It already intersects the Sugar River State Trail. All this trail development will make

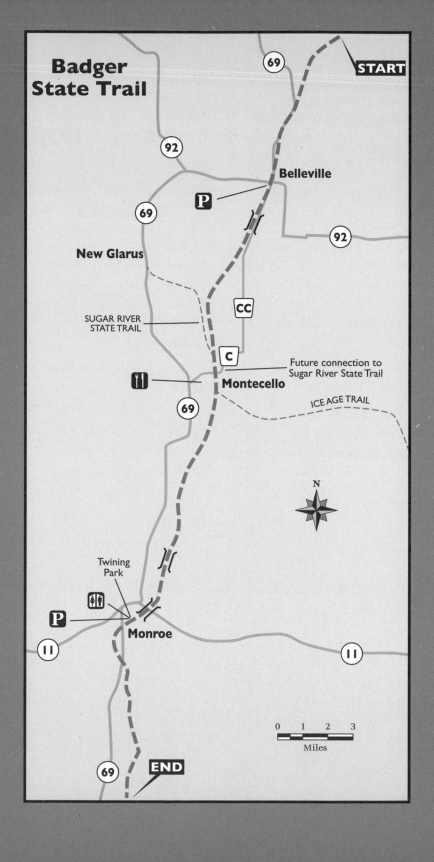

Badger State Trail

START

Belleville

New Glarus

SUGAR RIVER STATE TRAIL

CC

C

Future connection to Sugar River State Trail

Montecello

ICE AGE TRAIL

N

Twining Park

Monroe

END

0 1 2 3
Miles

this region of southern Wisconsin quite connected for bicyclists. For those wishing to venture farther, the Jane Addams Trail, beginning at the state border, continues to Freeport, Illinois, and connects into that state's own network of trails.

Don't just glance at a map to find your way onto the Badger State Trail. Be warned that Sun Valley Parkway leaving Paoli going east does indeed cross the trail—but at about 40 feet overhead. While the roughly 7-mile connection to Madison waits to be paved, your best bet is to start at the current trailhead where Purcell Road crosses the old rail bed 1.7 miles east of County Road PB just north of Paoli. The alternative is the possibly hair-raising experience of sharing WI 69 with speedy and frequent traffic for 1 mile south to Henry Road, where you can go east 0.3 mile and pick up the trail there as well. There are no parking lots at either of these trail entrances. In fact, the only official parking along the trail for now is in Belleville and at Twining Park in Monroe.

Starting from Purcell Road you will see immediately that though the trail passes through a lot of farmland, it is sheltered by trees on either side. The rail bed cuts through the earth here as you travel through mixed hardwoods. At 1.1 miles you will cross a bridge, the thirty-seventh of forty-one bridges on the trail, which are numbered starting at the Illinois border. You'll enter a mixed forest of oak-hickory, box elder, and stands of aspen. The rail bed sinks below the rest of the world and passes beneath the Sun Valley Parkway overpass at 1.6 miles.

At 2.5 miles cross another bridge, and then one more just 200 feet past it. At 2.8 miles you arrive in the one-tavern town of Basco. This is Henry Road, and a quarter mile to your right is WI 69. This is the connection to the alternative ride along the highway down from Paoli.

Just before you cross County Road A at 3.4 miles, you'll traverse another bridge, and at 4.0 miles, still another. From this point the trail rides just to the east of WI 69. It is exposed for a short distance and then crosses Frenchtown Road where partial shade resumes. At 5.1 miles there's a bridge as you approach the town of Belleville.

At 6.1 miles there is an exit off the trail to Fifth Avenue, where you can find Townmart, which sells refreshments as well as trail passes. At 6.6 miles you will cross an old steel trestle over the Sugar River. You'll enter Belleville crossing Main Street and Wisconsin Highway 92 at an angle. Main Street

The 1,200-foot Stewart Tunnel is located on the Badger State Trail.

offers some fast food, restaurants, and bars. To your right is Library Park, which provides picnic tables and restrooms when the building at the park center is open. If not, there are restrooms at the public library just past this on the trail. The lot behind the library offers parking, and there is a bike rack and self-pay tube for the trail pass.

At 6.8 miles cross Church Street and then Vine Street a block later. It is unshaded from here to the next bridge at 7.5 miles. To your left is a wetland area.

The trail crosses Fahey Road at 7.9 miles and continues south along County Road CC, crossing bridges at 8.5 and 8.8 miles. At 9.0 miles, at County Road W, New Glarus is 4.5 miles to the west on hilly county roads. At 9.5 miles cross County Road CC at an angle, and another 0.5 mile later cross another bridge. At 10.1 miles the trail hits Tunnel Road, and the woods start to thicken up around you.

Another bridge awaits, and then at 10.5 miles the rail bed burrows into the rocky hill and you are faced with the dark, gaping Stewart Tunnel. This 1,200-foot corridor is not lit, and a curve in its path prevents you from seeing the light at the end. If you're on a bike, it's best to dismount here and use a flashlight. The tunnel is named for the engineer who designed both the tunnel and the railway. The tunnel plays some fascinating games with sound. You may hear a low pulsing noise that might put a scare in some, but don't worry: It is actually the cooing of resident pigeons at the other end of the tunnel. The tunnel is short enough that the chill shouldn't disturb you. On hot summer days, in fact, it is a tremendous relief. You may occasionally be hit by dripping water; in the spring be careful of possible ice patches.

When you exit on the other side, you will find you are over 100 feet above the surrounding terrain, which drops away on either side beyond this hill. By 11.9 miles the land rises back up to the trail, and you cross Tunnel Road again at its southern end.

Cross Exeter Road at 12.2 miles and then Marshall Bluff Road at 12.6 miles. Watch for wild turkeys here. There's a marshy area on your right as you come up to another bridge at 13.0 miles. Two more bridges await at 13.8 and 14.2 miles, and then you come upon the largest of the bridges at 14.6 miles where the trail passes over the Little Sugar River for a nice view. At 14.7 miles, the trail is shaded again. A trestle crosses over the trail and also crosses the Sugar River State Trail, which is a short distance through the trees to your right. A connecting trail of about 30 feet is planned for a spot just past this trestle. These were competing railways. The Wisconsin and Southern were the most recent users of this line, while the Sugar River Trail once belonged to the Chicago, Milwaukee and St. Paul line.

At 15.0 miles cross County Road C. You can switch to the Sugar River Trail just 100 feet to your right if you'd like. The trail shows wetlands on either side of this stretch with some weeping willows. At 15.3 miles you can exit to the right to the town of Monticello. A grocery store offers snacks and a great deli.

The trail connects to County Road EE at 15.6 miles. To the right is the entry to the parking area at Monticello, where you'll find restrooms, water, a map board, and an old train depot that has been converted into a youth hostel. Those interested only in walking or riding through Stewart Tunnel find their best parking here. Also one can do portions of both the Badger and Sugar River Trails from this starting point.

Beyond County Road EE scenic wetlands await. From here to Monroe is 12 miles, and there are no facilities along the way. At 15.8 miles the Badger crosses the Sugar River Trail and continues south while the latter trail heads southeast. Another bridge crosses the smaller West Branch of the Little Sugar River at 15.9 miles and another seasonal creek at 16.3 miles. At 16.6 miles cross County Road F and then a bridge over Burgy Creek at 17.1 miles. When you pass Feldt Road at 17.6 miles, you'll ride through open hardwood woodlands, cross a bridge at 18.0 miles, and come to Gutzmer Road at 19.5 miles. Cross a bridge 500 feet past this.

Over 400 million years ago this was all under water, and you can see limestone formed by the sea bed in the ridges on either side of the trail. You will pass through a channel through the rock at 19.9 miles before crossing another bridge and Allison Road at 20.0 miles.

The farmland rolls away in all directions, and the trail takes on the charm of a country road offering more open spaces. You'll cross two more bridges at 20.7 miles and 21.7 miles before arriving at County Road FF at 21.9 miles. In July you can find black raspberries ("black caps") along the route. At 22.7 miles you'll pass over a road on a bridge and then cross Round Grove Road. At 23.0 miles you will find yet another bridge, and then at 24.8 miles you cross County Road DR as you enter the Monroe area. At 25.0 miles you must cross the divided Wisconsin Highway 11/81. Do this with caution.

Monroe is famous for its cheese, and there are many places to try some. It is one of the few places in the world that make limburger, and when you get a whiff of it you might understand why. It is an acquired taste, and there are some who swear by it. Your first cross street in Monroe is 22nd Avenue at 25.2 miles. You'll cross 18th Avenue, which is also Business WI 11, 0.3 mile later. At 25.8 miles is 14th Avenue, where you'll find Twining Park to the right. There is parking here as well as restrooms and water. A kiosk run by the Monroe Chamber of Commerce alongside the trail is sometimes occupied by a volunteer who can provide directions and brochures. Going left on 14th Avenue 2 blocks to 7th Street, left 2 blocks to 16th Avenue, and then right 2 blocks will take you to the picturesque town square and Baumgartner's, Wisconsin's oldest cheese store.

As you continue south on the Badger Trail from 14th Avenue, spur trails head right to the park and left to a commercial zone where there is a convenience store. At 26.2 miles you will pass over Eighth Street on a bridge and then Ninth Street at road level. To the right is a restaurant and gas station. From Monroe to the end of the trail, there are no places to stop for food, drink, or restrooms, so now's your chance.

Cross Tenth Street before attempting to cross WI 69. Use the cross-walks because traffic can come fast. You'll cross Sixth and Fifth Avenues just after the trail goes uphill moderately, one of the few obvious variations in the grade. From here the trail heads out of town on a long slow curve via some wetlands before it reaches 17th Street/Bethel Road at 27.1 miles. You'll cross a bridge and pass under a trestle still being used by trains and cross 21st Street at 27.3 miles.

The trail heads under WI 69 at 28.1 miles, then, it's smooth sailing to Clarno Road at 29.4 miles. From here trees and brush close in around the trail. You'll cross Melvin Road at 29.6 miles, Town Center Road at 30.6 miles, and Advance Road at 31.7 miles. Another bridge awaits 0.2 mile from there, and at 32.3 miles you will cross Schueyville Road and still another bridge.

The trail comes to County Road P after another bridge crossing at 32.8 miles where you will find Clarno. There is nothing here but a lumber company that may sell trail passes in the future. Two more bridges are left at 33.1 and 33.3 miles, and then you come to the Illinois state line at 33.8 miles. There is another 250 feet before the trail's end at Wuetrich Road/State Line Road, where you can find a bench at the trailhead of the Jane Addams Trail, which heads south to Freeport, Illinois. This trail is paid for with state tax money, so there is no use fee.

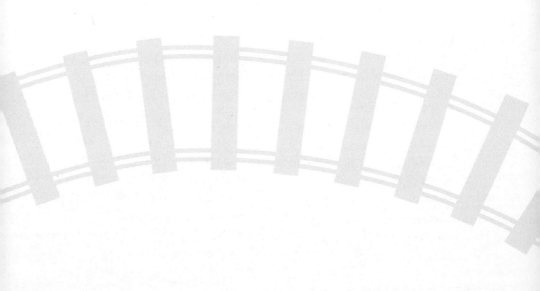

3 BEARSKIN STATE TRAIL

Ride from the thriving resort town of Minocqua into the heart of the Northwoods wilderness, enjoying scenic lake views and a fine city park near the Minocqua trailhead.

Activities:

Location: Minocqua to County Road K south of Harshaw

Length: 18.2 miles of rail trail, plus 0.2 mile of on-street and city trail in Minocqua

Surface: Finely crushed granite with wood-planked bridges

Wheelchair access: Yes

Precautions: Prepare for a very long distance between any services on the southern end of the trail. The last 9.3 miles are without any on-trail water or facilities. Mosquitoes are very common. Repellent is recommended for rest stops. Wisconsin State Trails have a carry-in/carry-out policy. Make provisions for carrying out any refuse. No trash receptacles are provided on-trail. A Wisconsin State Trail Pass is required for the Bearskin State Trail for bicyclists age sixteen and older ($4.00 daily or $20.00 annually). The trail pass also covers usage such as cross-country skiing, horseback riding, and bicycling on state mountain bike trails and other rail trails. Trail passes are available at BJ's Sport Shop on U.S. Highway 51 in Minocqua, the convenience store at the intersection of County Road K and US 51, and at self-pay stations at the northern and southern trailheads. In winter you must have a Wisconsin snowmobile registration or nonresident trail use sticker.

Food and facilities: Minocqua's Oneida Street (US 51) has numerous restaurants, fast-food places, and convenience stores. Hazelhurst has convenience stores and restaurants. There is a restaurant in Goodnow, 0.3 mile south of the trail on Lakewood Road. Flush toilets, showers, water, swimming, and a playground are at Torpey Park on the shore of Lake Minocqua, 2 blocks north of the trailhead. Water and pit toilets are at the South Blue Lake rest area, 8.7 miles south of the Minocqua trailhead, and at County Road K at the end of the trail.

Seasons: Open year-round

Access and parking: From US 51 in Minocqua (Oneida Street), turn west on Front Street and park in the municipal parking lot behind the post office. Or begin your trip from Torpey Park, two blocks north of Front Street on US 51. To access the southern trailhead from US 51, travel east on County Road K for 0.7 mile to the trailhead parking lot on the north side of the road.

Rentals: BJ's Sport Shop, (715) 356–3900. Z-Best Bikes, (715) 356–4224. Many hotels also rent bikes.

Contact: Wisconsin Department of Natural Resources, (715) 453–1263. Minocqua—Arbor Vitae–Woodruff Area Chamber of Commerce, (800) 446–6784 or (715) 356–5266, www.minocqua.org.

M inocqua is called the "Island City." It is accessible via a causeway from the north and bridges from the south and west. The western bridge was the route of the Milwaukee Road's famous Hiawatha passenger train. A trip on the Hiawatha revealed beautiful views of the town's shoreline as the train approached the depot. Today the view is reserved for the trail visitor.

Minocqua has all the earmarks of a tourist town. Shops and restaurants line its Main Street. One of my favorites is Hoorhay's, about 5 blocks south of the trail, for great coffee, tea, and the kind of healthy soups and sandwiches that don't make you feel deprived for being good. And if you want to be bad, there's ice cream, too. Just 2 blocks north of the trail is a wonderful little park with a swimming beach. Torpey Park gives the casual day-tripper a chance to enjoy the lakeshore just like people who come up and rent a cottage for a week. A city bike path goes from the park to the post office parking lot where the Bearskin Trail starts.

Going west from the Minocqua trailhead, the trail immediately begins by crossing a block-long railroad trestle. The view of Minocqua is wonderful, but it isn't your last. At 0.5 mile, after the trail has turned south, you cross another shorter bridge where you can see both the city and the first bridge.

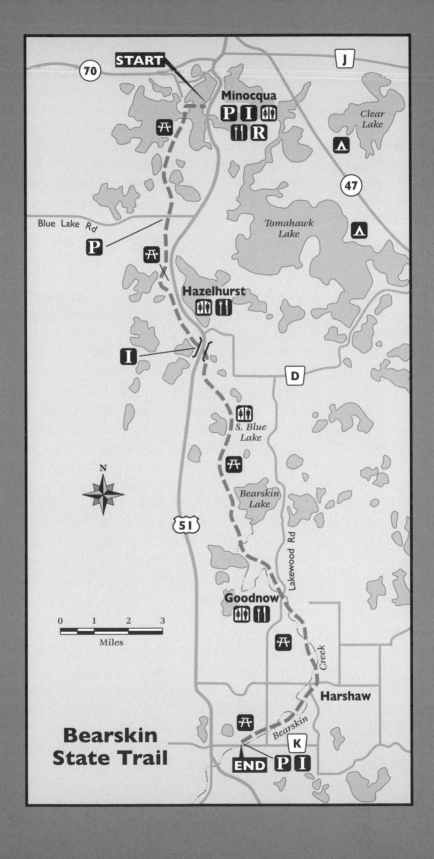

Trail bridges are great places to spot wildlife.

Nearly every mile of the trail that is not on a bridge is forested. Even the marshland you travel through after the second bridge is grown up with tamarack trees. The tamarack looks like an evergreen with its pointy tip and cone shape, but it drops its needles in the fall. It is usually one of the last trees to change color and one of the most beautiful. Coming upon a stand of the brilliant golden trees on a crisp fall day is thrilling.

The crossing of Blue Lake Road at 3.2 miles is marked only by a small parking area. If very young bicyclists are along, this is a great spot to be dropped off for a one-way trip back to Minocqua. There is an exciting feeling of discovery when kida see the city as they cross the bridges. Torpey Park makes a terrific destination, too. The playground and beach will make them feel the trip was worth all the pedaling.

At 5.1 miles you are on the edge of Hazelhurst, although you probably won't know it. The first road crossing after Blue Lake Road will be Oneida Street. A right turn (east) will take you 0.2 mile to US 51 where all of Hazelhurst's services are. Although you probably wouldn't hike or bike to it, it is also the location of the Northern Lights Playhouse, a semiprofessional theater that entertains with evening plays throughout the summer season.

An overpass bridge takes you across US 51, the only major road crossing along the trail. Say good-bye to signs of civilization. At 8.7 miles you come to the South Blue Lake rest area, where you will find drinking water. This is the last on-trail service. From there you plunge into the wilderness.

Wildness does equate with loveliness though. From Bearskin Lake on down you'll cross Bearskin Creek eight times. Each bridge is an opportunity to catch sight of waterfowl or perhaps a great blue heron. An observation deck looks out on the creek crossing at 12.3 miles, a spot where the stream spreads out to form a broad marsh.

At 13.2 miles you reach Goodnow. You'll find no town there anymore, but you can travel 0.3 mile south on Lakewood Road to the Pinewood Country Club, where lunches and dinners are served. Old Harshaw, at 15.6 miles, is no more a town today than Goodnow is, and there's no restaurant down the road. At 18.0 miles you arrive at the Spartan southern trailhead at County Road K, where you will find water and pit toliets. At 0.5 mile to the west, you can get trail passes and provisions at Northwoods Country Store where US 51 meets County Road K.

The state owns another 6 miles of trail heading south from here, but that section is undeveloped and only suited perhaps for mountain bikes and hikers.

Ojibwe Roots Grow Deep in Lake Country

No wonder the Highland Lake District of northern Wisconsin appealed to a canoeing nation like the Ojibwe. This Native American tribe came from the east, following a vision that told them they would find their new home where food grew on water.

The vision was realized when they reached the lakes surrounding Minocqua. Bays rippled with waves of grasses they had never seen before. Among the blades was a food that would sustain the tribe and become a choice part of dining in the area to this day. They called it menomin; we call it wild rice. The canoes they used were ideal for harvesting wild rice. Their narrow prows could easily slide into the grass.

The Ojibwe had found a paradise.

The birch bark canoe was perfect for traveling this lake region. The density of lakes here is a geographical phenomenon. Only three other areas on earth—parts of northern Minnesota, western Ontario, and Finland—have as much lake surface. With so many lakes, foot travel was very indirect. Canoes could be paddled in a straight line and then portaged to the next lake across narrow strips of land.

The Ojibwe's proficiency in building and paddling the birch bark canoe helped them form an alliance with the French in Quebec. They became an essential link in the main business of French Canada, harvesting animal furs for the fashions of Europe. The days of the fur trade were happy times. The tribe's history is wonderfully displayed at the Lac du Flambeau Chippewa Museum and Cultural Center on their Lac du Flambeau Reservation 12 miles northwest of Minocqua.

4 BUGLINE TRAIL

This is a surprisingly secluded trail in a sprawling metropolitan area. An active quarry and three parks en route add to the interest.

Activities:

Note: There is no special grooming for cross-country skiing.

Location: Menomonee Falls to Merton

Length: 13.7 miles, including the 0.3-mile River Trail in Menomonee Falls; 2.5-mile separate equestrian section from The Ranch in Menomonee Falls to Menomonee County Park; 4.4-mile section open for snowmobiling between Menomonee Falls and Sussex

Surface: Crushed limestone, wood-planked bridges; natural surface equestrian trail; asphalt paved on the Menomonee Falls River Trail section

Wheelchair access: Yes

Precautions: There are frequent crossings at busy roads, and possible washouts and soft surfaces on steep trail sections near the Lannon Quarry. Town streets must be used to connect east and west trail sections through Sussex. In winter you must have a Wisconsin snowmobile registration or nonresident trail use sticker.

Food and facilities: At the Millpond Park trailhead in Menomonee there is an open shelter, as well as water and flush toilets. All services, including bike retail and repair, are found in Menomonee Falls. Lannon has a drive-in right at the County Road Y trail crossing. There are a cafe and grocery in Sussex. All you'll find in Merton are a couple of taverns. Menomonee County Park has a playground, swimming beach, and flush toilets. Sussex Village Park has a playground and flush toilets. Lisbon Community Park has a playground and clean pit toilets.

Seasons: Open year-round

Access and parking: In Menomonee Falls at Main Street (Wisconsin Highway 74) and Grand Avenue, go north on Grand Avenue one-half block and turn right (east) into the parking lot behind the Associated Bank. Millpond

The Bugline Trail is popular with riders of all ages.

Park is on the east side of the lot. For a central jumping-off point or for horseback riding, park in Menomonee County Park (daily or annual vehicle parking sticker required) 1.5 miles north of Lannon on County Road Y. On the west, park on-street on County Road VV in Merton or at Lisbon Community Park, 5 miles west of Sussex on Lake Five Road (daily or annual vehicle parking sticker required).

Rentals: Emery's Bicycle and Fitness Center, Milwaukee, (414) 463–2453.

Contact: Waukesha County Park Department, (800) 366–1961. Waukesha County Tourism Initiative, (262) 548–7790.

What a nice trail to have in your backyard—literally. The Bugline Trail passes many backyards in Menomonee Falls, Lannon, and Sussex. Once satellite communities of Milwaukee, these towns are now part of the continuous urban/suburban mix. The surroundings are not all sprawl though. West of Sussex the trail gets into a real rural landscape. At the west end, the tiny village of Merton seems in no danger of being absorbed into the greater metro area.

What seems so surprising is the wonderful feeling of isolation along the trail, even at the housing-enveloped eastern section. Nice parks along the route are a big bonus, too. With the spacing of towns and parks, the longest distance between one or the other is less than 4 miles. The Bugline is a great trail for casual bicyclists or not-so-hard-core hikers.

The Bugline Trail connects to the asphalt-paved River Trail and Mill-pond Park in Menomonee Falls. This makes it possible to begin a trip from the east end right in the heart of downtown, next to the falls on the Menomonee River. Pleasant little Millpond Park overlooks the falls. If you are on a bike, you can begin riding just a few yards to the north.

Starting at Millpond Park, River Trail follows the river for 0.3 mile until it joins the Bugline Trail on the old railroad bed. Along the way, check out Classic Bike Shop on the corner of Roosevelt Road. It is really a "classic." It's what bike shops used to be like. In business since 1948, the owner has an incredible collection of bikes, which he displays in front of the shop on any nice day.

The Bugline Trail route (now on a crushed limestone surface) only stays on the rail bed until 0.6 mile before turning north and immediately coming out onto the cul-de-sac of Apple Tree Court, a residential street. At 0.7 mile the street reaches a T intersection with Shady Lane. Make a left turn (south) onto the sidewalk along the east side of Shady Lane. A half block farther, cross Appleton Avenue with the traffic lights, then turn right (northwest) and cross Shady Lane with the traffic lights. A left turn (southeast) onto the sidewalk along Appleton Avenue will take you back to the railroad grade Bugline Trail at 0.8 mile.

For a while you'll have a street or road crossing every block or so. Residents' backyards are just on the other side of the usually thick trees and shrubs. Keep an eye out for children. They seem to like darting onto the trail from little openings.

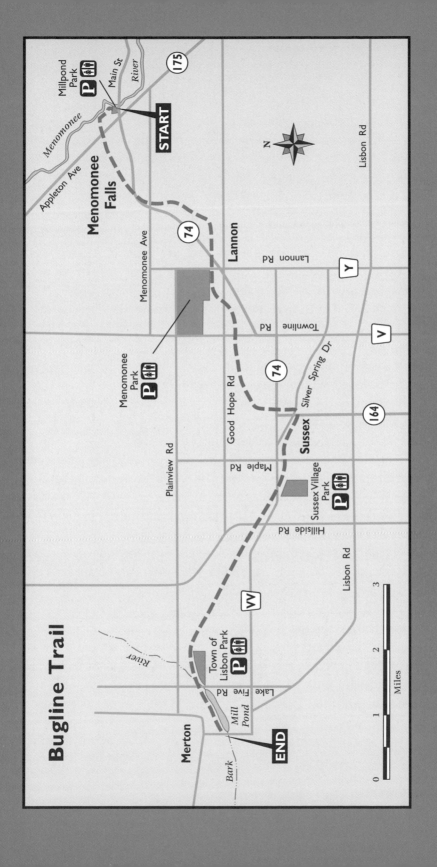

At 4.1 miles the rail bed begins to rise. It may seem strange to start shifting into the low gears on a rail trail, but the payoff comes as you round a bend for a great view of the huge open pit of the Lannon Quarry. The quarry is the reason the Milwaukee Road ran a rail line here in the first place. For decades "Lannon Stone," a fine limestone, has enhanced the beauty of buildings throughout the area.

The little village of Lannon is next at 5.1 miles. The trail just skirts the north edge of town, but the most desirable service, a cafe/dairy bar, is near the trail. At 5.4 miles a short spur trail leads to Menomonee County Park. This is a nice destination or a good place to take a break. A playground and swimming beach are a hit with kids.

The trail comes to an abrupt end at 8.2 miles on the outskirts of the small village of Sussex. Here it is necessary to ride on-street to reconnect with the rail bed trail. Direction signs for the on-street portion are very good. Begin by continuing south on Waukesha Avenue. At 8.4 miles you must cross busy Main Street (WI 74). Waukesha Avenue then becomes Wisconsin Highway 164. Continue south another 0.3 mile to the intersection with Silver Spring drive and turn right (northwest). Stay on Silver Spring drive for 0.4 mile then turn left (west) onto the rail bed.

As you head west out of Sussex, you pass Sussex Village Park on the south side of the trail. This typical town park has a playground and the luxury of aged shade trees. The trail now runs straight as an arrow in a northwestern direction for more than 3 miles. When it does bend to the southwest, a short spur trail at 12.4 miles takes you a few yards to Lisbon Community Park. This newer park has a modern playground, an open shelter, and a nice view of the course of the Bark River to the north. The shelter may be welcome on a hot day; the park's newly planted trees offer little shade.

At 13.0 miles the trail runs right next to the millpond backed up on the Bark River. When the millpond and the trail end at 13.7 miles, you are in Merton. The biggest attraction in this little village is the Merton Mill just across County Road KE and on the other side of the Bark River. The mill has all the noise, dust, and bustle that mark these fast-disappearing businesses. There is always a farmer on hand picking up feed or a local resident buying birdseed.

Plans are to extend the trail along the former Kettle Moraine railroad bed to the future Monches Park in North Lake.

5 CAPITAL CITY TRAIL

Access to Olbrich Gardens, views of the State Capitol, Lake Monona, and the Monona Terrace Community and Convention Center are highlights of the Capital City Trail. Soon it will connect to the Badger State Trail.

Activities:

Location: Madison

Length: 16.5 miles

Surface: Asphalt and concrete

Wheelchair access: Yes

Precautions: There are frequent street crossings on the eastern section of the trail and a crossing of busy Williamson Street in the downtown area. Pedestrian use may be heavy near the Monona Terrace Community and Convention Center. Short sections of the route are on-street. There are almost no on-trail services. As the trail heads south of the Beltline Highway, it becomes a state trail. For this portion, the Wisconsin State Trail Pass is required for bicyclists age sixteen and older ($4 daily or $20 annually). The trail pass also covers usage such as cross-country skiing, horseback riding, and bicycling on state mountain bike trails and other rail trails. You can purchase the pass at self-pay tubes at either end of the state portion of the trail. Lake Farm Park also sells passes and has a self-pay station.

Food and facilities: Madison offers a great variety of eating options. Several are near the Capital City Trail. The Sheraton Madison Hotel's Heartland Grill restaurant is just southeast of Olin-Turville Park. A half block southwest of John Nolen Drive and Williamson Street is the Essen Haus, a German-themed restaurant and beer hall (enter via the parking lot off of Blair Street, bike rack provided). For fine dining go 4 blocks northeast to Restaurant Magnus, which has an outstanding European and South American menu. There are flush toilets, open shelter, and water in Olin-Turville Park. Porta-type toilets are at the northeast end of the Monona Terrace Community and Convention Center. Flush toilets and water can be accessed at Olbrich Botanical Gardens.

Seasons: Open year-round

Access and parking: The closest parking lot to the trailhead is at Olbrich Park. Heading toward the Capitol in Madison on East Washington/U.S. Highway 151, turn left on Fair Oaks Avenue 0.4 mile east of the intersection of U.S. Highways 51 and 151. Take Fair Oaks 1.5 miles to Atwood Avenue. Go left on Atwood 0.7 mile to the parking lot on the right at the traffic light at Walter Street and Atwood. You can pick up the trail at Walter Street just 0.1 mile from the entrance to the lot. There are also parking lots at Olin-Turville Park, Lake Farm Park, and Dawley Park.

Rentals: Williamson Street Bike Works, (608) 255–5292, www.willybikes .com. Machinery Row Bicycles, (608) 442–5974, www.machineryrow bicycles.com. Yellow Jersey, (608) 257–4737, www.yellowjersey.org.

Contact: Greater Madison Convention and Visitors Bureau, (800) 373–6376, www.visitmadison.com. Dane County Parks, (608) 246–3896.

||||||||||||||||||||||||||||||||||||||||||||||||||||||||||||||||||||||||||||||||||||

M uch has changed on the trail over the years, and at times the names might get confusing. What was once the Nine Springs E-Way Trail is now an official segment of the larger Capital City State Trail, and only part of the trail is actually governed by the state and thus demands a trail fee. As the Madison network of multiuse trails grows, one hears more names for what was often just called the Capital City Trail—the Isthmus Bikeway or even the Monona Loop (a different route altogether now).

What you see on the map here is most likely the final look of the Capital City State Trail's pass through the city. It ends a short distance from the Military Ridge State Trail and connects to it by a partially on-road path that will be off-road in the future. It also connects to both ends of the Southwest Path: to the east end via Brittingham Path off John Nolen Drive and to the western terminus just east of Verona Drive. And if this wasn't enough of a web of excellent trails, then just wait for the final segment of the new 40-plus-mile Badger State Trail, which will soon part from a point near the western end of the Southwest Path and cross a bridge over the Capital City State Trail. When the eastern end of the Capital City Trail bridges that

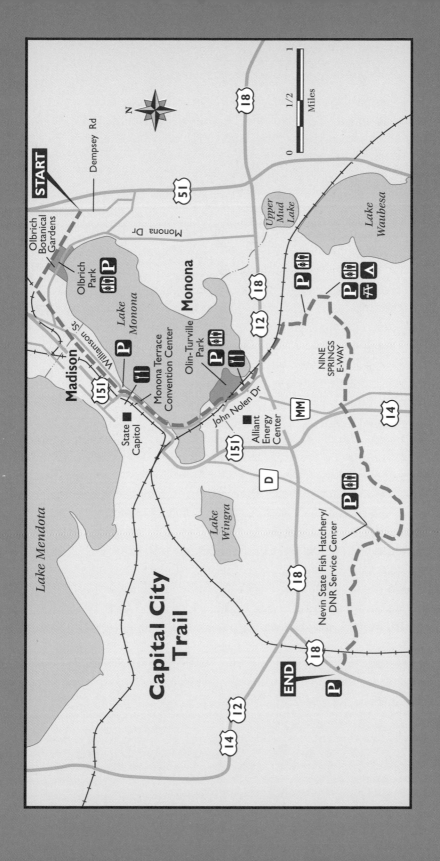

7-mile gap to Glacial Drumlin State Trail in Cottage Grove to the east, you will have an impressive trail indeed, connecting Waukesha to Madison, and extending to Illinois in the south and Dodgeville in the west.

Pick up the trail at Dempsey Road where it passes through residential neighborhoods alongside the tracks. At 0.7 mile you will cross the tracks at Walter Street, and then the tracks will be to your right. On the other side of Walter Street, a channel of water at the backside of Olbrich Park parallels the trail to your left. Watch to your left just before you reach the bridge over Starkweather Creek at 1.0 mile and you'll see the magnificent hand-painted Thai Pavilion. Cross the bridge and you can see Olbrich Botanical Gardens, also on your left. Both are definitely worth a visit.

The trail crosses Fair Oaks Avenue at 1.3 miles and 0.2 mile later parts from what was the Wisconsin and Southern line to go left on the former Soo Line. The next 0.5 mile continues through residential areas, and just before you arrive at Atwood Avenue, you will pass public gardens often burgeoning with flowers and vegetables in summer. At 2.0 miles cross Atwood at the light, where you'll touch the corner of the Harmony Bar—outstanding pizza!—and then cross Dunning Street to your right to pick up the paved trail again. The next stretch brings you through a narrow green space along Eastwood Drive where you will cross to your right at the traffic signal at 2.5 miles. There is a pedestrian crossing button you can press. On the other side the trail bears left, angling away from the busy street and crossing a steel bridge over the Yahara River. You'll cross a cul-de-sac here where the Yahara River Trail goes right along the river to Lake Mendota, passing under the busiest of the cross streets.

You continue straight across the street to pick up the trail, but only for another block. Once you reach Dickinson Street at 2.8 miles, the route follows East Wilson Street past the future Central Park until the street ends and the asphalt path resumes. The path takes you behind some Williamson Street businesses and then brings you to one of the busiest crossings at the intersection of "Willie" Street and John Nolen Drive at 3.8 miles. To your left is Bandung Indonesian Restaurant. Across Blair Street and heading toward the Capitol is the Essen Haus, a German beer hall complete with weekend polka bands. Your path, however, crosses Williamson, passing Machinery Row Bicycles on your left, and heads southwest, keeping John Nolen to your right and Lake Monona to your left. At 4.0 miles you will travel along

The Madison skyline and Lake Monona are part of the Capital City Trail scenery.

the concrete path between the Frank Lloyd Wright Monona Terrace Convention Center. Keep right on the path as there is always oncoming traffic; if you're walking, the lane closest to the water's edge is for you (and the many people fishing). The Monona Terrace is host to a variety of events and often live music. As fall progresses, the farmers' market moves indoors here as well.

Beyond the Terrace is the narrow Law Park, where the trail continues along the lakeshore. At 4.6 miles you will come to the T intersection where US 151/North Shore Drive intersects John Nolen. If you cross to your right at the light here, you will pick up Brittingham Path, which hooks up with the Southwest Path 0.3 mile to the west. But continue straight now, picking up the causeway that crosses Monona Bay. The views behind you of the Capitol dome and downtown reflected in the water show Madison at its finest, especially as sunset approaches.

The causeway stretches nearly 0.7 mile, and at 5.6 miles you will cross Wingra Creek. Another city trail goes right here and follows the creek all the way to the entrance to the Arboretum and Vilas Park and Zoo. From

The Frank Lloyd Wright Mystique

Frank Lloyd Wright set the world of architecture on its ear. Born in Richland Center, an hour west of Madison, Wright would make his home in nearby Spring Green. The home, Taliesin, was at first a refuge from the scandal that plagued him in Chicago, where he had made his mark at the end of the stodgy Victorian Era.

After honing his craft at the side of his mentor, Chicago skyscraper pioneer Louis Sullivan, Wright set out to destroy the "box," as he called it. In those days architecture was dominated by classical European forms. The facade was most important and how people lived inside was a poor second. He introduced new concepts of interior space and soon was designing unique homes for the city's elite through his own firm. Wright brought the outside in with the innovation of the picture window. He created the concept of indirect electric lighting, civilizing the harsh, new glaring bulb.

Wright left his family in Illinois and moved to Spring Green in 1911 with his lover, the wife of one of his wealthy neighbors. This might raise eyebrows even today; back then his actions railed against all that conventional morality stood for. And that was just the beginning. Before his death in 1959 Wright would survive more scandal and tragedy on his way to becoming the most prolific architect in the history of the world. Responding to a design competition in 1938 for a city/county administration building in Madison, he would set in motion an epic fifty-nine-year struggle in the budding state capital and university town to erect a publicly owned Frank Lloyd Wright building.

All of the resistance to what would eventually open as the Monona Terrace Convention Center in 1997 can't be laid at the feet of local conservative thinking and political sabotage. Wright was known for cost overruns and not paying his bills. He did his best to alienate about as many people as possible. A University of Wisconsin Art Department professor recalled organizing a faculty soiree in the 1950s to generate support for Wright's design. "You'd think he could just stick to the merits of the project," he recalled. "Instead he spent the whole time telling them all that was wrong with the university."

Approval of the Monona Terrace project would have to wait a long time. During this period Wright would continue to innovate and astound. The last structure he was to oversee the construction of was the Marin County Government Center in California. His Guggenheim Museum design in New York City astounded the world when it opened in 1959. In the meantime, Madison plugged along, bare of Wright-designed public buildings.

Wright's philosophical descendents, the Taliesin Fellowship, would pick up the banner and keep his Monona Terrace design alive through decades of referenda and rejection. Functional aspects of the building were modified to meet the needs of the times, but the stunning character of Wright's original design remained intact.

Opened in 1997, Monona Terrace quickly outstripped all income projections and changed Madison from flyover country to a unique destination city. The building was only the second publicly owned structure in the state designed by Wisconsin's famous son. The first was a unique one-room schoolhouse in beautiful Spring Green Valley that Wright built and donated for the benefit of area children.

Monona Terrace has a wonderful roof garden open throughout the day and into the evening. Reasonably priced guided tours of the building are offered daily. Call (608) 261–4000 for tour times or visit www.mononaterrace.com.

Wingra Creek the path continues along John Nolen Drive, passing Olin-Turville Park on your left and finally passing under U.S. Highway 12/18, The Beltline, at 6.7 miles. You will cross Nob Hill Road, where the trail becomes a state trail and the trail pass is required. Look for the self-pay tube or purchase one just down the trail at Lake Farm Park.

The trail heads southeast, crossing Raywood Road at 7.4 miles and then riding alongside it south 0.4 mile to Moorland Road, where it follows that street to the (left) east. At 8.1 miles you reach a parking area with restrooms across the road to your right at the same place where a boardwalk heads into the marsh to your left. You have arrived at Capital Springs State Park; the park entrance is at 8.5 miles. You can get trail passes here, and there are restrooms and water. The Lussier Family Heritage Center with its interpretive gallery tells stories of Dane County's natural, cultural, recreational, and community heritage.

From the park entrance the Capital City Trail crosses what was Moorland Road but is now Lake Farm Road after the bend behind you. The trail goes through the Nine Springs E-Way right across the south side of the city, where you will pass through prairie being restored to its original state and a bit of forest and oak savanna. The trail is exposed and from here loses its gentle grade now that you have departed from the former rail bed. The next 2 miles are without any road crossings until you reach County Road MM at 10.5 miles. Go straight across, then go right to cross McCoy Road. Bear left alongside it, cross the on-ramp to U.S. Highway 14, pass under the bridge, and finally get past the ramp on the other side. The trail resumes, and you'll follow alongside McCoy Road. At 11.4 miles the two diverge, and the trail passes through quiet woods and fields before heading uphill behind Eagle School to Gunflint Road at 13.1 miles. Follow this to Glacier Valley Road; the trail goes along the road 0.3 mile to Fish Hatchery Road. To your right is the Nevin State Fish Hatchery and an office for the Department of Natural Resources. There are restrooms and water here.

Go left on the asphalt path and cross the busy Fish Hatchery Road at the light, where you will pick up the path again at 13.7 miles. The trail goes up steeply, then curves to the right along the top of the small ridge before heading downhill. This next mile-long section follows a corridor shaded by oaks and a mix of other trees and crosses a couple of bridges over a seasonal creek that meanders between residential developments.

A short tunnel passes under Longford Terrace at 14.3 miles with ramps up to the roadway. You'll come back into the sun out of the trees at Edenberry Street. Cross a couple of open parks before arriving at Seminole Highway at 15.4 miles.

Dunn Marsh begins on the other side of the road. To your left is Dawley Park, which isn't much more than a parking area and offers no facilities. The trail is mostly exposed, though it passes through more mixed forest before you'll see an old railroad bridge over the trail at 16.1 miles, which will be the crossing of the Badger State Trail. Just beyond this and on the right-hand side, the Southwest Path links up. You will be able to go right here a short distance up the hill to find the entrance to the Badger State Trail in the future. The Capital City Trail continues from this intersection, passing a pond on the right, then a playground, and then another pond on the left before making the final climb up to the end of the trail on the access road along Verona Road at 16.5 miles. From here you can head left down to a short asphalt trail that takes you to the corner of McKee Road/County Road PD and Verona Road to find the Military Ridge State Trail trailhead 0.7 mile away.

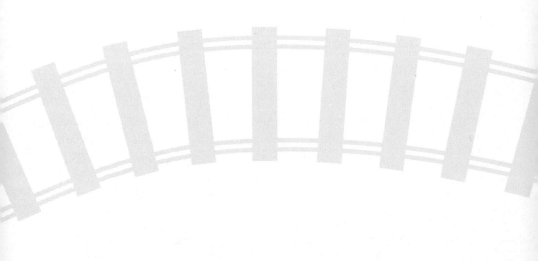

6 CHIPPEWA RIVER STATE TRAIL

Scenic highlights at broad river bends and lush bottomland forest await you on the Chippewa River State Trail. The trail connects to the Red Cedar State Trail via an impressive 860-foot-long trestle, as well as to the interesting City of Eau Claire Chippewa River Trail and Carson Park.

Activities:

Note: No special grooming is done for cross-country skiing.

Location: Eau Claire to the Red Cedar State Trail

Length: 27.6 miles, including 0.5 mile of city trail in Carson Park (connecting to another 4.1 miles of City of Eau Claire Chippewa River Trail) and 6.5 miles of Pepin County trail extending from the Chippewa River Bridge to Durand.

Surface: Asphalt with wood-planked bridges

Wheechair access: Yes

Precautions: Some trail sections have tended to wash out from flooding, creating rough, muddy crossings. Check ahead for the status of the trail. The only on-trail service is a country store in Caryville. The Eau Claire end of the trail is frequently busy with various types of trail users. Street crossings on the City of Eau Claire Chippewa River Trail require caution. The Wisconsin State Trail Pass is required for the Chippewa River State Trail for bicyclists and in-line skaters age sixteen and older ($4.00 daily or $20.00 annually). The trail pass also covers usage such as cross-country skiing, horseback riding, and bicycling on state mountain bike trails and other rail trails. Passes can be purchased at the bicycle shops in Eau Claire, Luer's Grocery in Caryville, and at a self-pay station at the Short Road crossing. In winter you must have a Wisconsin snowmobile registration or nonresident trail use sticker.

Food and facilities: All services are available in Eau Claire. Carson Park has a playground, water, snacks, an open shelter, and flush toilets. There is a Dairy Queen near the north end of the state trail. At the wayside park on Wisconsin Highway 85, you'll find an open shelter, water, and clean pit toilets. There is a country store in Caryville and clean pit toilets in the trail parking lot. In Meridean you will find a soft-drink machine outside of an old garage. The Durand trailhead has parking, camping, portable toilets and a swimming pool near the parking area.

Seasons: Open year-round

Access and parking: From Interstate 94 take the Wisconsin Highway 37/85 Eau Claire/Mondovi exit and travel north 1.2 miles to U.S. Highway 12 (Clairmont Avenue). Turn left (northwest), travel 0.4 mile to Menomonie Street, turn right (east), and travel 0.2 mile to Carson Park Drive. Turn left (north) and continue 0.4 mile to the parking lot on the left (north) side of the drive in back of the baseball stadium.

Rentals: Riverside Bike and Skate, (715) 835–0088

Phone numbers: Chippewa Valley Convention and Visitors Bureau, (888) 523–3866 or (715) 831–2345. Wisconsin Department of Natural Resources, (608) 266–2621. Pepin County Tourism, Durand, (715) 672–5709.

The Chippewa River State Trail begins in the interesting city of Eau Claire and plunges deeper and deeper into the wilds of the river valley. The City of Eau Claire Chippewa River Trail offers a terrific 4-mile loop that allows access to the cafes, taverns, and bike shops on Water Street and the attractions of Carson Park. You can enjoy the best of the city and the country on these trails.

In the late nineteenth-century, Eau Claire was "Sawdust City." Nine companies operated twenty-two sawmills in the valley. In 1884 they processed 800 million feet of timber. As the water in the Chippewa rose each spring, log drives brought the winter's harvest downriver at the rate of a million feet an hour. Half Moon Lake, which surrounds Carson Park, was a storage area for the forest's bounty.

Carson Park is an excellent starting point for a Chippewa River State Trail ride. Although the state trail lacks a true trailhead, the city trails have a great one in Carson Park. There are parking and facilities, of course, but

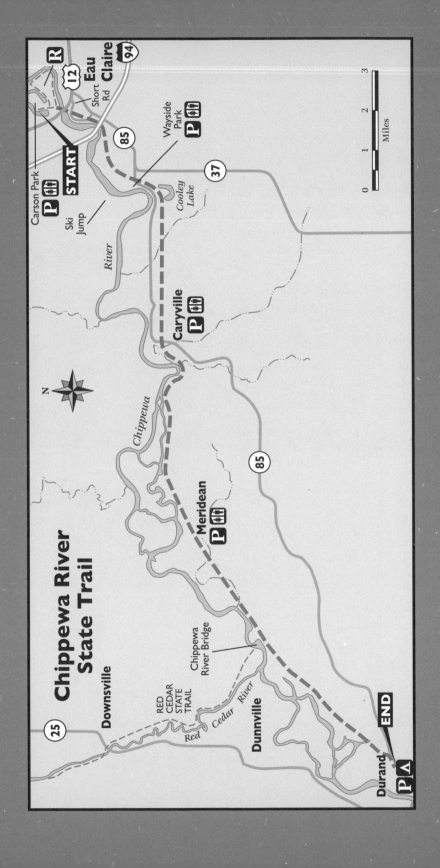

Chippewa River State Trail

Eau Claire

R

12

Short Rd

94

START

85

Carson Park 🅿 👫

Ski Jump

Wayside Park 🅿 👫

37

Cooley Lake

River

Caryville 🅿 👫

N

Chippewa

85

Meridean 🅿 👫

25

Downsville

RED CEDAR STATE TRAIL

Chippewa River Bridge

Red Cedar River

Dunnville

END

Durand 🅿 ⛺

0   1   2   3
Miles

the beautiful setting and the attractions are the real draw. In front of the solidly built limestone baseball stadium is a statue of home run slugger Hank Aaron, who began his pro career here in the minor leagues. Next door, the Chippewa Valley Museum displays the heritage of the area, from the Native Americans to early city life. There is a re-creation of Paul Bunyan's logging camp and even a working early-twentieth-century ice-cream parlor.

Beginning at Carson Park, travel south on the paved trail on the opposite (east) side of Carson Park Drive from the parking lot. After passing through a beautiful stand of pines, the trail runs closely parallel to Carson Park Drive and descends steeply before junctioning with the City of Eau Claire Chippewa River Trail at 0.5 mile. A left turn (east) would take you on a 4.1-mile loop through the city on a nicely designed paved trail that follows a railroad grade to the Chippewa River, then travels through riverside parkland to the big Chippewa River State Trail iron bridge. The City of Eau Claire Trail is very scenic with many interpretive historical markers.

Continuing south on the trail parallel to Carson Park Drive, you come to the end at a T intersection with Menomonie Street about 40 yards farther. There is a Dairy Queen on this corner to your left. Turn left (east) and either follow Menomonie Street or the sidewalk in front of the Dairy Queen for about 40 yards to the northern end of the Chippewa River State Trail and turn right (south). At 0.7 mile you come to a split in the trail. Go left to stay on the Chippewa River State Trail and cross the iron bridge over the Chippewa River. (To the right the trail swings east, passes under the bridge, and becomes the City of Eau Claire Chippewa River Trail.)

At 0.8 mile you reach the south shore of the Chippewa River. The trail immediately passes under the US 12 bridge. Almost instantly, you'll feel you've left the city behind. At 1.5 miles you cross Short Street, which is the beginning of the part of the trail where the State Trail Pass is required. There is a self-pay station at this point. The trail passes under I–94 at 2.0 miles and under WI 85 at 4.2 miles. Just before the underpass of WI 85, a short spur trial splits off the right to a wayside park at a scenic bend in the Chippewa River.

The WI 85 wayside park is a nice place to take a break. Across the river you can see the impressive profile of the Silver Mine ski jump rising 351 feet above the river level. The Eau Claire Ski Club built the modern jump in 1969, but ski jumping has been a winter sport in the area since 1887.

The Chippewa River: "The Road of War"

The fur trade, the first European contact for many Native Americans, brought manufactured goods like steel knives, brass pots, iron traps, firearms, brass hawk bells, glass beads, and silver ornaments far into the interior of the continent. The trade made life less difficult and more colorful. Hunting and trapping to harvest furs for exchange became much more efficient. Constructing dwellings and canoes was quicker and easier.

Most Midwestern tribes remember the fur trade era as a happy time, a time of plenty. The French fur traders didn't want their land; they came to the great rendezvous each year with their gifts. They accepted the furs in exchange, celebrated with their Native American friends, and were gone.

But the trade often put tribes in conflict with each other. The equilibrium that had existed between human and game populations was shattered. A tribe involved in the fur trade could, and had to, live off five times the amount of land as they had before contact. They needed more land to get more furs. Eastern tribes, armed by the fur traders, pushed their western neighbors farther west. Western tribes strove to get into the fur trade to obtain similar goods, and the pressure was repeated on the tribes farther west.

Once in the fur trade, the tribes couldn't go back to the old ways. They couldn't make iron tools, guns, and gunpowder for themselves, and they couldn't survive without them. War was inevitable: There is no clearer example than the 150-year conflict between the Ojibwe (Chippewa) and the Dakota (Sioux).

According to legend, the Ojibwe came from the seacoast. The Dakota once lived in the Upper Peninsula of Michigan and northwest Wisconsin. By the early 1700s the Ojibwe had pushed them across to the Mississippi River and down into southern Minnesota. The Chippewa River became a highway for war canoes, allowing the Dakota to penetrate the interior of the Northwoods where the Ojibwe reigned. The Ojibwe, in turn, could quickly paddle to the Chippewa outlet at Lake Pepin, part of the Mississippi, in the heart of Dakota territory.

The entire region around the Chippewa River was a no-man's-land. Early settlers barricaded themselves inside cabins and sawmills, becoming bystanders as the wars raged. The last battle, a three-day affair, took place near Eau Claire in 1854. Henry Wadsworth Longfellow's epic poem *The Song of Hiawatha* was based on an Ojibwe story of how the love of the brave Hiawatha and the Dakota maiden Minnehaha brought peace to the two tribes.

At 5.4 miles you'll see Cooley Lake on the south side of the trail. The lake is an abandoned oxbow bend of the Chippewa River. The trail now passes through farmland, although the grown-up brush and trailside trees provide some shelter from the sun. At 6.7 miles you cross a town road. This area was once the village of Lufkin; now it is just a couple of houses.

The trail reaches Caryville at 10.3 miles. There, Luer's Grocery is your last chance to pick up food or supplies. At 11.4 miles you follow a nearly 180-degree bend in the river. Other good river views come at 12.6, 13.6, 14.7, and 16.1 miles. At 16.7 miles you pass a handful of houses that are all that remain of the little village of Meridean (pronounced *Merry-deen* by the locals).

At 19.7 miles the trail begins a mile-long stretch alongside the river. At 21.1 miles you reach the junction with the Red Cedar State Trail. Turn right (north) and travel 0.1 mile for a fine view of the 860-foot iron bridge over the Chippewa.

You can continue north on the Red Cedar State Trail to Downsville, 6.7 miles away, or to the city of Menomonie and the northern trailhead at 14.2 miles. The Chippewa River State Trail continues another 6.5 miles to Durand. This segment, however, is maintained by Pepin County.

Hank Aaron's statue looks out over Carson Park.

From the Red Cedar State Trail juncture, the trail begins a slow climb out of the river's floodplain. At 23.0 miles you will cross a perennial stream and make your first crossing of County Road M 0.2 mile later. County Road M lies in your path again 0.7 mile farther as you pass through prairie. From there the trail descends into hardwood forest, and you eventually cross a Class II trout stream known as Bear Creek, and soon after that, Little Bear Creek.

From this point you'll see farmland spread across the floodplain as the trail rises to Durand. You'll enter town at Tarrant Park, where you'll find restrooms, water, a swimming pool, and campgrounds. This may be a good stopping point; otherwise the trail's end is another 0.5 mile into downtown, ending at Main Street.

7 ELROY-SPARTA STATE TRAIL

This is an exceptionally beautiful trail with the added interest of three railroad tunnels along the route. Five pleasant trail towns are oriented toward "trail tourism" and cater to all types of users. Located in the heart of an Amish settlement area, the trail is linked to two other rail trails at Elroy and one other at Sparta.

Activities:

Location: Elroy Commons in Elroy to the Sparta Depot in Sparta

Length: 34.0 miles, including 0.5 mile of "400" State Trail and an on-street route in Elroy, and 2.5 miles of on-road route and La Crosse River State Trail into Sparta.

Surface: Crushed limestone with wood-planked bridges

Wheelchair access: Yes

Precautions: Bicycles must be walked through each of the trail's three tunnels. Flashlights or bike lights are recommended. All tunnels are much cooler than outside. The third tunnel is nearly three-quarters of a mile long and is likely to take fifteen minutes to a half hour to walk through. It also has a small waterfall spring in the middle. Caps and windbreakers or long-sleeved shirts are recommended. Wisconsin State Trails have a carry-in/carry-out policy. Make provisions for carrying out any refuse. No trash receptacles are provided on-trail. The Wisconsin State Trail Pass is required for bicyclists age sixteen and older ($4.00 daily or $20.00 annually). The trail pass also covers usage such as cross-country skiing, horseback riding, and bicycling on state mountain bike trails and other rail trails. Passes can be purchased at Elroy Commons, Kendall Depot, Judy's Trail Cafe in Norwalk, the Sparta Depot, at many area businesses, and at self-pay stations at trail parking lots. In winter you must have a Wisconsin snowmobile registration or nonresident trail use sticker.

Food and facilities: Numerous restaurants and fast-food places are near the trailhead in Sparta. Cafes are in Wilton and Elroy, while a convenience store and two taverns can be found in Kendall. There are swimming pools in Sparta, Wilton, and Elroy, and playgrounds at Norwalk, Wilton, Sparta, and Elroy. Water and flush toilets are at the Sparta and Kendall Depots, Norwalk Town Park, Wilton Village Park, and at Elroy Commons. Water and pit toilets are at the east end of Tunnel #3 and at the northwestern trail terminus. There are showers at Elroy Commons.

Seasons: Open year-round

Access and parking: For the eastern trailhead, take the Wisconsin Highway 82/Mauston exit from Interstate 90/94 and drive west 13 miles to Elroy. The Elroy Commons trailhead is between Main Street (Wisconsin Highway 80/82) and Railroad Street just north of Franklin Street (County Road O). For the western trailhead, go north 0.2 mile from the Wisconsin Highway 27/Sparta exit off I–90 and turn right (east) on Avon Road. Go 0.7 mile to South Water Street and turn left (north). Go 0.3 mile to Milwaukee Street and park at the Sparta Depot. Shuttle service is offered by the Kendall Depot in Kendall, Speed's Bicycle Sales and Service, and the Franklin Victorian Bed & Breakfast in Sparta. A wide variety of on-trail and on-road bicycle tours is offered by Speed's.

Rentals: Speed's Bicycle Sales and Service, Sparta, (608) 269–2315. Elroy Commons, Elroy, (608) 462–2410 or (888) 606–BIKE, www.elroywi.com/el-roy.htm. Kendall Depot, Kendall, (608) 463–7109, www.elroy-sparta-trail.com. Tunnel Trail Campground, Wilton, (608) 435–6829. Margaret's Market/Main Street Market, Wilton, (608) 435–6517.

Contact: Elroy-Sparta State Park Trail Headquarters, Kendall Depot, (608) 463–7109, www.elroy-sparta-trail.com. Elroy Commons Bike Trails and Tourist Information, (608) 462–2410, www.elroywi.com. Sparta Area Chamber of Commerce, (608) 269–4123 or (888) 540–8434, www.spartachamber.org.

A million bicyclists or more may have used the Elroy-Sparta State Trail in its thirty-plus years of existence. With a typical yearly usage of more than 60,000 persons, the math works out. Well, a million bicyclists can't be wrong; this is one great trail.

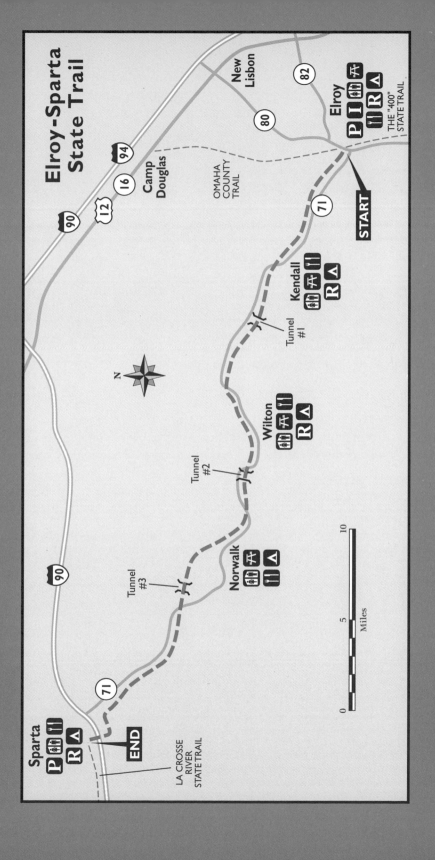

Elroy-Sparta State Trail

Bicyclists emerge from the long tunnel between Sparta and Norwalk.

The three tunnels are adventures in themselves. Although they are too tricky to ride through and must be walked, it doesn't diminish the experience. Walking makes the passage even more enjoyable. Just be sure you don't have any problems with claustrophobia before taking on Tunnel #3 between Norwalk and Sparta. It took three years to build this 3,810-foot-long marvel. Light at the end of the tunnel can't always be counted on. When hot and humid summer days arrive, so much mist forms around the entrances that they seem completely black when you are in the middle.

Tunnel #1, between Kendall and Wilton, and Tunnel #2, between Wilton and Norwalk, are more manageable. At 1,680 feet each (about 0.3 mile) they are a lot less intimidating. With temperatures in the 50- to 60-degree range, all the tunnels are great places to cool down on hot days. Caps and windbreakers or long-sleeved shirts will keep you from getting chilled.

The town of Elroy has become quite the rail trail center. The comfortable restored railroad buildings at Elroy Commons serve three trails that intersect in town. The Elroy-Sparta State Trail is linked to the "400" State Trail to the south and the Omaha Trail to the north. A cafe just across Railroad Street from the commons buildings offers food service right at the trailhead.

Heading north from Elroy Commons, follow the extension of the "400" State Trail for 0.2 mile until a T intersection at Cedar Street. Turn left (west) and go 0.3 mile to the intersection of WI 80/82 and Wisconsin Highway 71. Cross WI 80/82 and begin riding on the Elroy-Sparta State Trail on the northeast side of WI 71. Brown and white direction signs do a good job of guiding you to the trail.

The 6.4-mile section between Elroy and Kendall is quite open. The Baraboo River Valley is very wide here, and the high bluffs are off in the distance. This stretch is a good chance to get to know the river—you'll cross it seven times. As you near Kendall, the valley begins to narrow, giving the town a pleasant New England village appearance. The restored Kendall Depot is always a gathering spot for trail riders seeking a rest and a little shade.

Traveling west from Kendall, the trail follows the Baraboo River for several miles before crossing it one last time. Turning into a narrow side valley, the rail grade steepens slightly and enters a deep cut in moss-covered limestone bedrock. At 10.0 miles you arrive at the giant 20-foot-high entrance of Tunnel #1. On a hot day you can feel the cool tunnel air before you can see the entrance.

As you walk into the tunnel, darkness slowly envelops you. After about 50 yards, what seemed a large space changes to a black void, with the bright outline of the far entrance in the distance and a faint glow of the tunnel walls alongside. This is where a flashlight or bike light comes in handy. You could make it through without one, but seeing the trail surface in front of your feet helps.

Leaving the tunnel, the scenery is reversed from the approach. Now it opens up before you, ever widening as you travel westward. The Tunnel Trail Campground at 11.7 miles is a wonderful little private campground with a swimming pool. At 13.3 miles the trail overpasses WI 71 on a special modern bridge and enters the valley of the Kickapoo River. At 15.4 miles you are at the crossing of County Road M in the village of Wilton. At this point signs direct you along the streets to the village park, where a swimming pool is always a great place to cool off on a hot day. Each summer Sunday morning the local Lions Club serves a pancake breakfast in the park.

West of Wilton, at 17.7 miles, Tunnel #2 is close to a carbon copy of the first tunnel. The tunnel approach is different, though, as the trail runs

The Nation's First Rail Trail

In the early 1960s, Stan Solheim had a problem. While working on a new Wisconsin State Outdoor Recreation Plan, he'd been wondering if bicycling might become a popular form of recreation in the future. He thought railroad rights-of-way would make great biking corridors. Put enough of them together and you could ride all the way across the state. But everytime he brought up the idea of including bicycling in the plan, he ran up against the same problem: How can you plan if you can't show any demand?

Fishing, boating, and camping were all easy to plan for. Thousands of people enjoyed them each year in Wisconsin, but too few people bicycled to produce any usage figures. Then one day Ralph Hovind, Stan's boss at the Commercial Recreation Development Bureau, said, "Stan, you've been talking about biking on railroad grades. Here's one in the paper that's for sale."

The Chicago and Northwestern Railroad wanted to sell its old line between the towns of Elroy and Sparta in west-central Wisconsin. The asking price was $12,500. The 32-mile section had three tunnels along its length; the longest had cost more than a million dollars to bore in 1873. The sale price seemed like a bargain. In 1965 the Chicago and Northwestern pulled up the rails and the Commercial Recreation Development Bureau convinced the Wisconsin Conservation Department (WCD) to buy it.

The WCD, predecessor of today's Wisconsin Department of Natural Resources, first set up the Elroy-Sparta State Trail for hiking. Then, in 1966, the Bicycle Manufacturer's Association (BMA) in Chicago, under the direction of Bob Cleckner, organized a cross-state publicity ride that included the Elroy-Sparta State Trail. Solheim, Cleckner, and University of Wisconsin Extension Agent Larry Monthey laid out the rest of the route between La Crosse on the Mississippi and Kenosha on Lake Michigan on lightly traveled rural roads. They called it the Wisconsin Bikeway.

"Cleckner brought in some hard-pedaling European riders," Solheim remembers. "When they got to the Elroy-Sparta they just kept going right over the old cinder base. The BMA made sure the ride had good newspaper coverage and the demand I thought was out there began to materialize. Calls started coming in for information about the Wisconsin Bikeway and particularly the Elroy-Sparta Trail. When people rode the trail they complained about the old cinders though."

In 1967 the WCD experimented with special surfacing for bicycling on a 1-mile section north of Elroy. "They used finely crushed limestone," Solheim said. "It was actually the screenings—waste product—from a gravel crushing operation. It was the cheapest thing they could get, but it worked very well."

When the trail season began in 1968, another 10 miles had been surfaced, and demand kept going up and up. By 1971 more than 23,000 registered riders enjoyed the trail's scenic, motor vehicle–free bicycling experience. In 1975, 42,500 riders used the trail.

Today the Elroy-Sparta State Trail is linked to three other state trails, forming a nearly continuous 100 miles of rail trail. Only about 50 miles of trail gaps remain in a planned 250-mile cross-state rail trail system. More than 60,000 people now visit the Elroy-Sparta State Trail in a typical season, and the Wisconsin Department of Tourism gets more than 100,000 requests for information on bicycling annually. How's that for demand?

The Elroy-Sparta Trail tunnels are always an adventure for kids.

closely parallel to WI 71, gradually climbing higher and higher above the road level before the highway curves from the trail as you approach the tunnel entrance. Breaks in the trailside trees and brush allow occasional glimpses of the highway; otherwise the trail seems very isolated. At 20.8 miles the trail passes through Norwalk along the village park.

Tunnel #3, at 24.1 miles, is a true wonder. It represented state-of-the-art engineering when it was completed in 1873. The result is still amazing. Nearly three-quarters of a mile long, the tunnel was bored through solid rock from both ends and the middle. That's right, the middle. A shaft was sunk from on top of the hill for ventilation and to enable workers to dig toward the ends.

In winter huge wooden doors at each end of Tunnel #3 were closed between trains to keep ice from building up inside. Today the doors are still closed in winter, and snowmobiles follow a trail over the hilltop. A light and a windbreaker or warm shirt are necessities rather than conveniences for a walk through this tunnel. The far entrance, which was such a bright, reassuring light in the shorter tunnels, is a tiny dot, if visible at all. Fog can obliterate it for most of your trip through on a hot day. That also means that once you are in the middle, little or no light is visible at either end. The sound of a little waterfall in midtunnel adds to the strangeness of the experience.

You may not have noticed the gradual 150-foot climb from Norwalk to the east entrance of Tunnel #3, but you'll really feel the descent from the west entrance. You'll lose that 150 feet in a little over a mile. On a bike you'll feel like you're flying as the valley opens before you and the trail overpasses WI 71.

At 32.3 miles the rail bed trail ends, and you must follow back roads and streets for 1.0 mile to connect to the La Crosse River State Trail and the Sparta Depot. From the trail parking lot, ride 0.4 mile west on Imac Avenue to a T intersection with Igloo Road. Turn right (north) and go 0.6 mile into Sparta to the La Crosse River State Trail on the west side of the road, which has become John Street. Take the trail for 0.7 mile to the Sparta Depot. A trail bridge over I–90 is being planned to connect the Elroy-Sparta State Trail into town without the detour.

Sparta is very proud of the trail. The city bends over backward to cater to trail visitors. An example of their pride is in a little park 5 blocks north of the Sparta Depot at South Water Street and Wisconsin Street East (U.S. Highway 16). Billed as "The World's Largest Bicycle," a colorful fiberglass sculpture of a rider on an old-fashioned high-wheel bicycle makes a great photo opportunity.

For another unique bicycle attraction, go 2 more blocks north on North Water Street and 1 block west on West Main Street to the Deke Slayton Memorial Space and Bike Museum, which honors hometown astronaut Deke Slayton and displays a collection of unique bicycles. You'll see everything from iron-wheeled bone shakers to the no-nonsense mountain bike local rider Olga McNulty rode to win Alaska's on-snow Iditabike race.

The Sparta Depot is also the location of the Sparta Tourism Bureau, a clearinghouse for all sorts of information on area services and events, and it is the jumping-off point for the La Crosse River State Trail, which continues west for 21.5 miles where it joins the Great River State Trail.

8 THE "400" STATE TRAIL

The "400" is a pleasant trail with many river crossings and five towns en route. The easternmost link of a 100-mile rail trail system, it's near Wisconsin Dells, one of the state's most popular tourism destinations.

Activities:

Location: Reedsburg to Elroy

Length: 22.0 miles, with 7.5 miles of separate equestrian trail between La Valle and Wonewoc

Surface: Crushed limestone with wood-planked bridges; grassy natural surface on the equestrian trail section

Wheelchair access: Yes

Precautions: Use caution on the La Valle to Wonewoc section, which has separate horse and bike/pedestrian trails. Soft spots and occasional wash-outs and potholes may be found on the crushed stone surface. Wisconsin State Trails have a carry-in/carry-out policy. Make provisions for carrying out any refuse. No trash receptacles are provided on-trail. The Wisconsin State Trail Pass is required for bicyclists and equestrians age sixteen and older ($4.00 daily or $20.00 annually). The trail pass also covers usage such as cross-country skiing and bicycling on state mountain bike trails and other rail trails. Passes can be purchased at the Reedsburg Depot Visitor Center, the Trail Break Cafe in La Valle, Elroy Commons, at area businesses, and at self-pay stations at trail parking areas. In winter you must have a Wisconsin snowmobile registration or nonresident trail use sticker.

Food and facilities: Many fast-food restaurants are on Wisconsin Highway 33 on the east side of Reedsburg. Cafes and convenience stores are in all trail towns. Indoor shelter, wheelchair-accessible flush toilets, and water are found in Reedsburg at the Depot Visitor Center. Wheelchair-accessible flush toilets and water are at the trail parking lot in La Valle. Horse trailer parking, pit toilets, and trail access are 1.5 miles east of the intersection of County Road G and WI 33 in Wonewoc. Open shelter, wheelchair-accessible flush toilets, and water are at Baker Field in Wonewoc and at the trail parking lot in Union Center. Open shelter, indoor shelter, a modern playground, wheelchair-accessible flush toilets, showers, and water are at the Elroy Commons trail parking lot in Elroy. Wheelchair-accessible flush toilets and water are at the trail parking lot in Hillsboro. Swimming pools are in Reedsburg, Wonewoc, Hillsboro, and Elroy. A swimming beach is at Lake Redstone County Park, 2 miles east of La Valle.

Seasons: Open year-round

Access and parking: From Interstate 90/94 in Wisconsin Dells, take Wisconsin Highway 23 16 miles west to Reedsburg. In Reedsburg the trailhead is at the Depot Visitor Center at Railroad Street between Walnut Street and Park Street, 1 block south of WI 33/23. Or, from I–90/94 in Mauston take Wisconsin Highway 82 13 miles west to Elroy. In Elroy the trailhead is at the Elroy Commons between Main Street (Wisconsin Highway 80182) and Railroad Street just north of Franklin Street (County Road O).

Rentals: Depot Visitor Center, Reedsburg, (800) 844–3507 or (608) 524–2850. Elroy Commons, Elroy, (608) 462–2410 or (888) 606–BIKE (2453).

Contact: "The Depot" in Reedsburg, (800) 844–3507 or (608) 524–2850, www.reedsburg.org. Elroy Commons Bike Trails and Tourist Information, (888) 606–2453 or (608) 462–2410, www.elroy.wi.com.

T he lazy, meandering Baraboo River snakes through the beautiful bluff country between Reedsburg and Elroy. In a canoe you'd have to paddle more than 40 miles to cover the distance. The "400" State Trail takes a more direct approach, cutting the length to 22 miles. The Chicago and Northwestern Railroad's famous "400" streamlined train was always in a hurry along this stretch. Much of the scenery you'll soak up at bicycle, hiking, or horseback speed was just a blur to the passengers. Lucky you.

When you visit, you can take the time to linger in small towns that were just a long horn toot for the "400" train. There will be no reason not to pause at one of the eleven crossings of the Baraboo River or to stop for a better look at a pair of squawking sandhill cranes. A 4-mile side trip

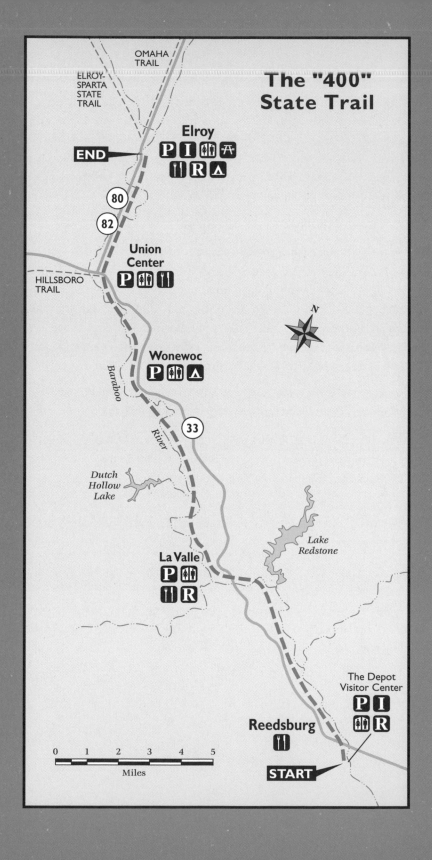

Rock formations line the trail near La Valle.

to Hillsboro on the Hillsboro Trail is not out of the question for leisurely travelers. After all, you wouldn't want to come this far and miss the "Czech Capital of Wisconsin." Each year on the second weekend of June, the little community trots out its ethnic pride at the "Cesky Den" celebration, polka dancing from dawn to dusk.

At the Elroy end of the "400" State Trail, you can connect with two other rail trails. The 12-mile Omaha Trail runs north to Camp Douglas on I–94. The 32-mile Elroy-Sparta State Trail heads northwest and connects with other trails that can take you up the Mississippi River.

Another plus for the "400" is that all of its pastoral quiet is only a few miles from Wisconsin Dells. The "Dells" has been a tourist attraction for well over a century. Visitors first came for boat excursions through the fascinating rock formations, the Dells, along the Wisconsin River. You can still enjoy a boat tour. All of the pristine natural beauty of the river has been preserved.

Today the Dells is as well known for its other attractions. Water parks, both outdoor and indoor, lure families for a day of splashing and relaxing. At Tommy Bartlett's Robot World you can step inside the Russian

When Passenger Trains Ruled

During the heyday of passenger rail travel, three railroads competed for the lucrative Chicago-to-Minneapolis business. Speed was the key to success, and the train's style affected its speed. The 1930s saw the introduction of streamlined passenger trains with lightweight aluminum bodies and sleek art deco designs that mimicked the aerodynamics of airplanes. The Burlington Northern had its famed Zephyr. The mighty Hiawatha sped along the Milwaukee Road.

The "400" State Trail rail bed belonged to the Chicago and Northwestern Railroad. It was here the "400" train ate up the tracks as it streaked to Minneapolis. Pulled by one of the first diesel locomotives, it was truly state-of-the-art technology. The Chicago and Northwestern sales pitch guaranteed coverage of the 440-mile run in less than 400 minutes. Where the rail line ran straight, the engineers would run the train at speeds in excess of 100 miles per hour.

Space Station Mir for an instant dose of claustrophobia. Yes, it is a real Mir, identical to the one that hosted various international crews of three for thirteen years. The tiny cylinder was their home for months at a time.

If you begin your ride in Reedsburg, take a little time to visit the shops on Main Street, just a block from the depot trailhead. This is what Main Street used to be like in so many American towns: a thriving, pleasant place to shop or dine. Try the Deli Bean Cafe for a great muffaletta sandwich, coffee, and enough choices of cheesecake to make your head spin.

Heading west from the depot, at 0.2 mile you come to the only significant road crossing on the trail, Main Street (WI 33) in Reedsburg. The first 8 miles of the "400" State Trail run in the broadest part of the Baraboo River Valley. Dense tree and brush along the rail bed keep you shaded. For several miles the trail runs right next to the river channel. Near the outskirts of La Valle, at 6.9 miles, you'll go through an underpass of busy WI 33 as the trail winds among picturesque rock formations. La Valle, at 8.0 miles, is one rocky town. Some houses are built right on top of the stone. The town is tiny, but the hospitality at the Trail Break Cafe makes up for it. The little restaurant next to the trail parking lot caters to visitors, serving food from snacks to pizza.

The 7.5-mile section between La Valle and Wonewoc is the trail's most unique stretch. You will bridge the Baraboo River five times along the way. Just west of La Valle, at 8.3 miles, the trail passes the edge of lily pad–covered Hemlock Lake. Farther on, it runs close to the southwest side of the river valley. There you will find a different climate as the sheltered north-facing rock formations foster white pines and other trees and plants more commonly found far to the north. This is also the section with a special equestrian path alongside the trail.

In Wonewoc, at 15.5 miles, the trail runs behind the buildings of Center Street, the town's main drag. Wonewoc Legion Park, with its swimming pool and playground, is at the north end of town, just a block off of Center Street. On the 4-mile stretch to Union Center, the trail again runs close to the Baraboo River.

Entering Union Center at 18.4 miles, just before the "400" State Trail crosses WI 33, the Hillsboro Trail splits off to the left. The 4-mile-long Hillsboro Trail is a pleasant side trip that follows the course of Branch Creek. Just before reaching Hillsboro the rail grade runs along Sanford Field, dedicated to Hillsboro's Josh Sanford. In the days leading up to World War II, Sanford flew more than one hundred missions over China with the Flying Tigers.

In Union Center the "400" State Trail parallels the town's business district 1 block to the east. A playground is located at the trail parking area. The 4-mile section between Union Center and Elroy is the most open stretch, running close along WI 80/82. As you approach Elroy at 20.9 miles, Schultz Park with its swimming pool and playground is just across the highway. Staying on the trail, you will end up at Elroy Commons, the northern trailhead, at 21.7 miles. The restored railroad buildings are always a center of activity. The actual northern end of the trail is at 22.0 miles, 3 blocks north of Elroy Commons at Cedar Street, where signs direct you to the Omaha Trail and Elroy-Sparta State Trail.

9 GANDY DANCER TRAIL

The Gandy Dancer has a nice mix of woodlot, farm, marsh, and lake scenery, with frequent services at nine communities along the trail. An exceptionally scenic state park is near the southern trailhead, and the St. Croix National Scenic Riverway is near both ends. There is a fascinating reconstructed trading post near the north end.

Activities:

Location: St. Croix Falls to Danbury

Length: 47.1 miles

Surface: Asphalt for the first 1.4 miles north of the Polk County Information Center near St. Croix Falls, then mainly crushed limestone with wood-planked bridges

Wheelchair access: Yes

Precautions: The grade is steep for the first 0.5 mile north from the Polk County Information Center near St. Croix Falls. Wisconsin State Trails have a carry-in/carry-out policy. Make provisions for carrying out any refuse. No trash receptacles are provided on-trail. The Wisconsin State Trail Pass is required for bicyclists age sixteen and older ($4.00 daily or $20.00 annually). The trail pass also covers usage such as cross-country skiing, horseback riding, and bicycling on state mountain bike trails and other rail trails. Passes can be purchased at the Polk County Information Center near St. Croix Falls, the Burnett County Department of Tourism in Siren, and at numerous local businesses. In winter you must have a Wisconsin snowmobile registration or nonresident trail use sticker.

Food and facilities: Numerous restaurants and fast-food places are in St. Croix Falls and in Taylors Falls on the Minnesota side of the St. Croix River. There are cafes in St. Croix Falls, Taylors Falls, Milltown, Luck, Frederic, Webster, and Danbury, and there are taverns in all trail towns. Flush toilets and water are at the Polk County Information Center near St. Croix Falls, Centuria town park, Anderson Field in Milltown, and Village Park and Soo Line Depot/Frederic Historical Society Museum in Frederic. Pit toilets are at Butternut Lake Park in Luck, Elbow Lake Wayside Park between Lewis and Siren, Crooked Lake Park in Siren, and Jeffries Landing Park between Webster and Danbury. There is swimming at Interstate State Park, Butternut Lake Park in Luck, Crooked Lake Park off the trail in Siren, and Ralph Larrabee Park just south of Danbury. Playgrounds are at parks in Milltown, Luck, Frederic, and Siren.

Seasons: Open year-round

Access and parking: From the U.S. Highway 8/Wisconsin Highway 35 intersection near St. Croix Falls, go south 0.2 mile to the Polk County Information Center.

Rentals: Wissahickon Farm Country Inn provides bikes for hotel guests, (715) 483–3986. Eric's Bike and Canoe Rental, St. Croix Falls, (651) 270–1561, www.ericsbikeandcanoe.com.

Contact: Burnett County Department of Tourism and Information, (800) 788–3164 or (715) 349–5999, www.burnettcounty.com. Polk County Information Center, (800) 222–POLK (7655) or (715) 483–1410, www.polkcountytourism.com. Wild River Outfitters, (715) 463–2254, www.wildriverpaddling.com.

Gandy dancing anyone? The trail's unusual name is linked to its railroad history. It seems that work crews who spent their days maintaining the line used tools made by the Gandy Tools Company. They frequently worked in unison to a vocal or mechanical beat as they pounded spikes or pried rails. Their laborious ballet earned them the name "gandy dancers."

Today the old Minneapolis, St. Paul and Sault Ste. Marie rail bed is the scene of pleasant recreation rather than hard work. The frequency of parks and small towns en route keeps a trip on the Gandy Dancer from ever seeming too strenuous. The longest distance between towns or parks is only 6.6 miles. The rail bed runs near WI 35 for much of its distance, but has a very isolated feel thanks to the thick brush and tree growth along the trail. It is a haven for birds at any time and a great place for spotting migratory waterfowl heading for nearby Crex Meadows Wildlife Area in the spring and fall.

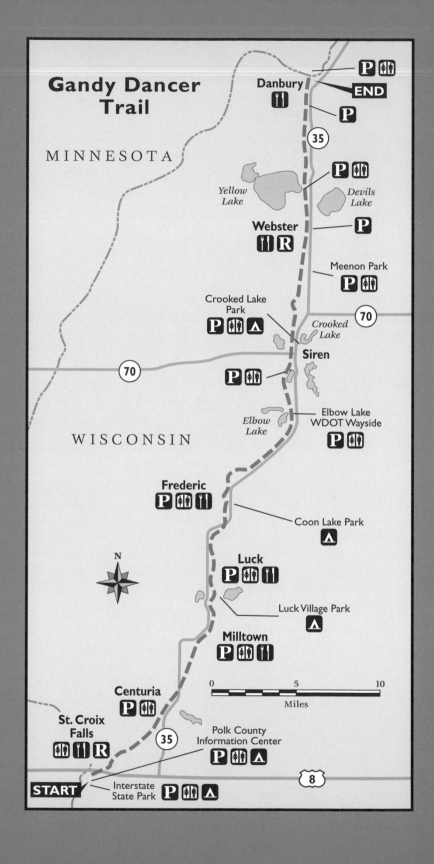

The Polk County Information Center near St. Croix Falls makes an ideal jumping-off point. It is also a great place to learn about the area's many attractions. The view of the St. Croix River is one of the not-to-be-missed experiences. The towns of St. Croix Falls and Taylors Falls are laid out on the steep valley sides of the Wisconsin and Minnesota shores of the St. Croix River. Both towns are treasures of beautiful nineteenth-century architecture. The lumber industry made the towns prosper, and builders certainly didn't skimp on wood. The view of Taylors Falls has a New England–like character, especially at fall color time. Its historic district of Greek Revival homes and churches amid a stand of tall maple trees on the valley edge is one of the finest examples in the Midwest.

Two hundred miles of shore along the St. Croix and its tributary, the Namekagon—from the river's headwaters to its confluence with the Mississippi—are preserved from development by the St. Croix National Scenic Riverway. The stretch north from St. Croix Falls is little changed from the days of the birch bark canoe and the log drive. Wild River Outfitters, 20 miles west of the trail where Wisconsin Highway 70 crosses the St. Croix, has a campground and offers canoe and kayak trips and shuttle service on the most pristine parts of the river. For a scenic but less private and less physical river experience, you can board one of the Taylors Falls Scenic Boat Tours, which ply the waters of the lower gorge each day.

A spur trail from the Polk County Information Center runs south, parallel to WI 35, for 0.3 mile to the entrance road of Interstate State Park. Near the entrance you can visit the Ice Age Interpretive Center, where you'll learn about the dynamic processes that created the park's spectacular scenery. One exhibit shows how the park's unique potholes were formed: When the St. Croix River burst through ancient layers of lava, whirlpool-trapped boulders bored into the rock. One pothole is 80 feet deep. The best way to enjoy the scenery is to hike one of the park's many trail loops, ranging from 0.3 to 1.6 miles in length. On your hike, it's likely you'll see people climbing on the steep, jagged cliffs. Interstate Park is very popular with rock climbers, who are great fun to watch.

Beginning at the Polk County Information Center, the Gandy Dancer State Trail winds up the valley side for 1.4 miles to the beginning of the rail bed. The trail is asphalt here, and for a short, 0.2-mile stretch is routed on a quiet street before going through a tunnel under US 8. By the time

There's room for everyone on the Gandy Dancer Trail.

you reach the tunnel, you will have climbed 170 feet. At 1.2 miles a spur trail splits off to the bluff-top residential streets of St. Croix Falls. When you reach the rail bed at 1.4 miles, the surface becomes crushed limestone.

Farther on, the trail cuts cross-country, tracking northeast through surrounding farmland. At 4.5 miles the trail passes the west edge of the little village of Centuria, which celebrated, appropriately, its first one hundred years in the year 2000. The town park has a little playground if you have children along who need a break.

Leaving Centuria, the trail runs parallel to WI 35 on its west side for 2.0 miles before crossing to the east and setting its own course for Milltown. At 10.7 miles the trail skirts the east side of Milltown, passing Anderson Field, a ballpark that also has swings and a slide.

At 14.4 miles the trail passes the west side of the town of Luck. All services are off the trail, but a side trip one-half block east on Butternut Avenue to Main Street is worth it just for a stop at the Luck Bakery. Big Butternut Lake Park is a lovely spot a mile farther east.

The 6.1-mile section between Luck and Frederic is one of the longest stretches between towns on the trail. It is also one of the most scenic, with five stream crossings. In Frederic, at 20.3 miles, you can visit Village Park in a nice setting on Coon Lake, 3 blocks east of the trail on Linden Street. Trail-side, 1 block north of Linden Street at Oak Street, is the Soo Line Depot/ Frederic Historical Society Museum, where local history and the story of the railroad days are exhibited.

At Lewis, at 25.7 miles, the only service you will find is a roadside tav-ern. North of Lewis you venture into lake country. The trail skirts the edge of Elbow Lake at 27.9 miles. There is a wayside park along WI 35 that can be accessed at this point. Farther north the trail passes the shore of Clear Lake just before arriving at Siren, at 31.4 miles.

Siren has two motels. One of them, the Best Western Northwoods Lodge is also the location of the Burnett County Department of Tourism and Information office. Crooked Lake Park makes a good rest stop, but must be accessed by going east across WI 35 on Main Street, then north 6 blocks on Fourth Avenue.

At 38.0 miles you enter Webster, a community that thrives on the tourism drawn by resorts on the many area lakes. North of town, at 41.1 miles, you'll visit one of them, Yellow Lake. Jeffries Landing is mostly a boat launch area on Yellow Lake, but a picnic bench makes it a good spot to take a break and enjoy the view.

Between Webster and Danbury, 2.7 miles west of the trail on County Road U, is Forts Folle Avoine Historical Park. Located near the banks of the Yellow River, this living museum of the fur trade era is on the actual site of the trading post and Ojibwe village. The history for most of the years of European contact in this part of the nation was not about lumberjacks and settlers. For 200 years a relationship called the fur trade existed between the French in Quebec and Native Americans of the western lakes and riv-ers. These times are re-created at Forts Folle Avoine just as they might have been in 1802.

At 46.6 miles the trail passes Ralph Larrabee Park on Round Lake, another good spot to sit for a while and feel the lake breeze. At 47.1 miles you reach the Wisconsin trailhead in Danbury. The trail actually continues on for another 51 miles, through Minnesota and back into Wisconsin to the city of Superior. There is no special development on this section though, and it is more popu-lar for off-road motoized vehicles. Danbury shed some of its sleepy river town image with the opening of the Hole in the Wall Casino and Hotel, owned by the St. Croix band of Ojibwe. Happy days are here again.

10 GLACIAL DRUMLIN STATE TRAIL

You'll experience a variety of scenery, from rolling glacial hills to vast marshes to great rivers, along the Glacial Drumlin State Trail. Also of note: a glacial lake, a bison herd, and five crossings of a lazy meandering stream. The trail is near the Kettle Moraine State Forest and the ancient Native American village at Aztalan State Park.

Activities:

Note: There is no special grooming for skiing, but groomed trails are located in the Kettle Moraine State Forest units and at Cam-Rock County Park in Cambridge.

Location: Waukesha to Cottage Grove

Length: 52.4 miles, including 1.0 mile of city trail in Waukesha and 2.0 miles of on-road route between Helenville and Lake Mills

Surface: Asphalt for 12.9 miles from Waukesha to Dousman; crushed limestone with wood-planked bridges for the rest of the trail

Wheelchair access: Yes

Precautions: At 10.0 miles, the trail deviates from the rail bed for 1.3 miles and follows the natural terrain contours. These contours are mostly gentle, but there is a short steep section at 10.6 miles. There are few services along the 25.6-mile section between Sullivan and Deerfield. There is a grade-level crossing of busy U.S. Highway 18 between Sullivan and Helenville. A 2.0-mile section between Helenville and Lake Mills is on-road. There are several busy grade-level highway crossings. The trail is mostly open with occasional shaded stretches. The use of sunblock is advised. Wisconsin State Trails have a carry-in/carry-out policy. Make provisions for carrying out any refuse. No trash receptacles are provided on-trail. The Wisconsin State Trail Pass is required for bicyclists and in-line skaters age sixteen and older ($4.00 daily or $20.00 annually). The trail pass also covers usage such as cross-country skiing and bicycling on state mountain bike trails and other rail trails. Passes can be purchased at the Bicycle Doctor along the trail in Dousman, the Glacial Drumlin State Trail Headquarters at the Lake

Mills Depot, at numerous trail-town businesses, and at self-pay stations at trail parking lots. In winter you must have a Wisconsin snowmobile registration or nonresident trail use sticker.

Food and facilities: Numerous restaurants and fast-food places are found in Waukesha, although none are near the trailhead. There is a restaurant just west of Wales. Cafes or restaurants are in Dousman, Sullivan, Jefferson, Lake Mills, Cambridge, Deerfield, and Cottage Grove. Taverns are in all trail towns except Wales. A country grocery in Sullivan is popular with trail users. Flush toilets and water along the trail are at the eastern trailhead at the Fox River Sanctuary in Waukesha, in Wales, Dousman, Sullivan, Glacial Drumlin State Trail Headquarters at the Lake Mills Depot, and Deerfield. The Lake Mills Depot also has showers. Pit toilets and water are at Aztalan State Park, 1.7 miles north of the trail between Helenville and Lake Mills. Water is at the McArthur Road crossing, 1.0 mile west of the eastern trailhead, and at Pohlman County Park between Sullivan and Helenville.

Seasons: Open year-round

Access and parking: From US 18 in Waukesha, go southwest for 0.7 mile on County Road X (St. Paul Avenue) and turn left (south) on Prairie Avenue. Go 0.4 mile and park in the lot at the Fox River Sanctuary at College Avenue and Prairie Avenue. For the western trailhead, from the Interstate–94/County Road N exit, go south 2.3 miles to Cottage Grove and the Glacial Drumlin State Trail parking lot.

Rentals: The Bicycle Doctor, Dousman, (262) 567–6656.

Contact: Cambridge Chamber of Commerce, (608) 423–3780, www.cam bridgewi.com. Delafield Chamber of Commerce, (262) 646–8100, www .delafield-wi.org. Glacial Drumlin State Trail Headquarters-West, (920) 648–8774. Glacial Drumlin State Trail Headquarters-East, (262) 646–3025. Jefferson Chamber of Commerce, (920) 674–4511, www.jefnet.com/jeffer son. Lake Mills Area Chamber of Commerce, (920) 648–3585, www.lakemills .org. Waukesha Area Tourism Council, (800) 366–8474 or (262) 542–0330.

As you might guess from its name, the Glacial Drumlin Trail traverses terrain formed by the last continental glacier. This monstrous ice sheet descended from Canada, and it covered the entire northern tier of the United States until it began melting about 12,000 years ago. One of four glaciers in the last million years, it was named the Wisconsin Stage because most of its distinct characteristics were identified here. A visit to the Glacial Drumlin State Trail is a trip through some of its most fascinating and beautiful features.

Paralleling I–94 and US 18, the trail is easily accessed at many points. Kettle Moraine State Forest units near the eastern end offer scenic hiking and camping opportunities. Most interesting of all, perhaps, is Aztalan State Park, a remnant of a Native American civilization that disappeared 700 years ago.

If you begin your trip in Waukesha, take some time to explore this interesting small city. Downtown streets are lined with ornate Victorian storefront buildings. The streets converge at a spot called the "five points." The streets were laid out on Native American trails, resulting in this unusual pattern. Today a reproduction of a springhouse stands at this point. Pure spring water made Waukesha famous in the days when it was the alternative to demon rum.

At the Fox River Sanctuary in Waukesha, you'll notice on-street bike route signs leading to the east. These take riders to another rail trail, the New Berlin Trail, which goes from the west edge of the city to the eastern edge of Milwaukee.

Heading east from the Fox River Sanctuary on the city trail that leads to the Glacial Drumlin State Trail, you cross the Fox River at 0.2 mile on an impressive old iron railroad trestle. At 0.5 mile the trail passes under busy Wisconsin Highway 83. Soon the terrain around the trail begins to change character. Gently rolling hills give way to steep roller-coaster hills as you enter the Kettle Moraine. Here the Green Bay and Lake Michigan lobes of the glacial ice sheet ground against each other, and huge blocks of ice became buried in the earth. When they eventually melted, the ground above sank, making deep kettle-shaped depressions. Many filled up with water, creating lakes and bogs.

You'll see some of the best scenery in the state as the trail winds along, seeking the easiest passage through the moraine. At 6.2 miles a

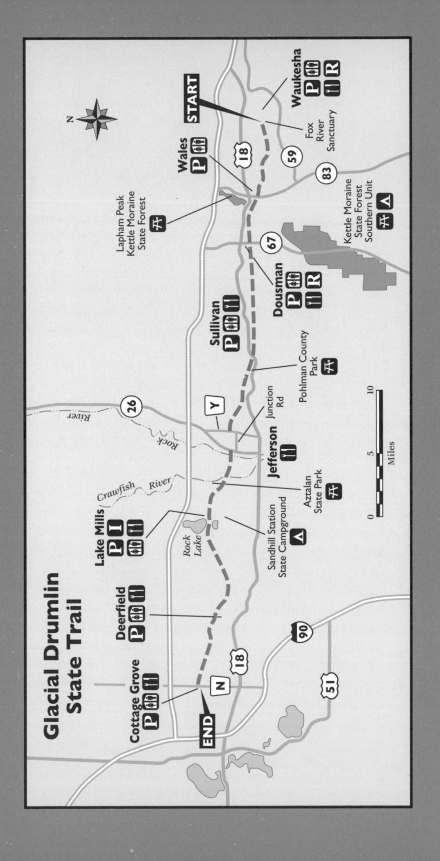

Glacial Drumlin State Trail

N

Waukesha
START
Fox River Sanctuary

Wales
18
59
83

Lapham Peak Kettle Moraine State Forest

67

Kettle Moraine State Forest Southern Unit

Dousman

Sullivan

Y

Pohlman County Park

26

River

Rock

Crawfish River

Junction Rd

Jefferson

Lake Mills

Aztalan State Park

Rock Lake

Sandhill Station State Campground

Deerfield

90

Cottage Grove

18

N

51

END

0   5   10
Miles

little wooden bench on the north side of the trail looks out on a gorgeous view of the oak-forested Kettle Moraine hills. Shortly, the trail enters "the big cut," a mile-long cut that deepens until it reachs 50 feet at a wooden overpass bridge near Wales. The sides of the cut bloom with wildflowers throughout the spring and summer and brighten with patches of red sumac in the fall.

At 7.5 miles you reach the little village of Wales. Settled by the Welsh, the town is the high point of the trail, 180 feet higher than the Waukesha trailhead. All the town services moved out to the highway after the feed mill burned down a decade ago. Still, the village green is a pleasant place to take a break. Heading west out of Wales, you pass under Wisconsin Highway 83; less than a half mile later you'll see Saxe's restaurant on the north side of the trail at the Mickel Road crossing. This is the only trailside service between Waukesha and Dousman.

Dousman, at 12.9 miles, may not be much bigger than Wales, but it does have more accessible services. The Bicycle Doctor is right next to the trail, as is a small town park with a playground. A cafe and grocery are just a half block north of the trail on Main Street. The town was originally called Bullfrog Station, and as you head west you'll find out why. Gone are the forested Kettle Moraine hills; ahead is the vast Bark River Marsh, stretching for 3 miles. With a swamp that big, frog croaking can get downright obnoxious.

At 18.7 miles the trail visits another tiny village. Sullivan is a real trail town. It withered on the vine after the railroad was abandoned and the interstate highway drew the traffic off of US 18. Trail users and local farmers bring in most of the business these days. The corner grocery store, 2 blocks north of the trail on County Road E, always welcomes trail travelers.

Now comes a long lonely stretch. The trail doesn't seem too far off the beaten path for a while. For the first 4 miles, it closely parallels US 18, crossing from the south to the north side along the way. Then, just past a little wayside park with a picnic table and water pump, the trail curves to the northwest. On the map it looks like it passes close to Helenville. Although it does, the rail bed passes under Helenville Road, so most trail users bypass the town because they would have to travel a section of US 18 to get to it.

At 27.5 miles the rail bed trail ends at a T intersection with County Road Y. In order to rejoin the trail, you must turn left (south), go 0.3 mile to

The bridge at Rock Lake is a pleasant spot for a rest stop.

Junction Road, and turn right (west). At 28.9 miles you'll pass Dewey Road, which runs off to the south. Dewey Road offers a lightly traveled 2.4-mile route into Jefferson if you are in need of services. There are a cafe and a tavern in downtown Jefferson, but most of the services are along Wisconsin Highway 26 on the south side of town.

Traveling west on Junction Road, you'll see huge grain elevators ahead on the right. These belong to an ethanol plant. At 30.2 miles, just before Junction Road T intersects with WI 26, the Glacial Drumlin State Trail resumes with a short spur trail that runs north along the highway for 0.3 mile to rejoin the rail bed and pass under the state highway.

Now the trail's story becomes one of big rivers. Immediately after going under WI 26, the trail crosses the broad Rock River on a long trestle. For thousands of years the Rock was the river highway to the Mississippi for Native American canoes. Local burial mounds point to associations with the Hopewell culture, an Ohio-based civilization that thrived in the early years of the first millennium.

At 32.9 miles you'll come to another river crossing. This is the Crawfish River, which joins the Rock nearby at Jefferson. Interpretive signs on the bridge tell about the Middle Mississippian culture's village upstream and point out one of their remaining fish weirs. Weirs are lines of rock set in the river to funnel fish into a narrow space where they can be caught easily.

At 33.3 miles the trail crosses County Road Q, which has a paved shoulder. At this point you can take a 1.7-mile side trip north to the village site at Aztalan State Park. One of Wisconsin's most significant archaeological sites, Aztalan was a fortified village and the northernmost outpost of the Middle Mississippian culture. For almost 300 years, from about A.D. 1000 to 1300, the village was part of a vast trading network centered near St. Louis. Distinctive flat-topped pyramidal ceremonial mounds mark their sites. Recent archaeological discoveries suggest that people moved here from the St. Louis area to found the settlement.

Back on the Glacial Drumlin Trail, the stretch between County Road Q and Lake Mills is one of the most sheltered. In some spots you'll pass through a tunnel of trees. You'll reach the Glacial Drumlin State Trail Headquarters at the Lake Mills Depot at 36.7 miles. The depot is a popular rest stop, with its indoor shelter, restrooms, showers, trail museum, and outdoor deck. At this point you can access downtown Lake Mills by going north on Main Street (Wisconsin Highway 89) for 1.1 miles. The town has a shaded village green with a bandstand. Daily specials and homemade soups at Cafe on the Park on Main Street make it a favorite stop for trail users.

From the Lake Mills Depot you can also access the Sandhill State Campground. This sixteen-site rustic camping area on the shore of Mud Lake is a haven for sandhill cranes. The cranes are among the most ancient of birds, and their squawking call has an eerie, primeval quality. To get to the campground from the depot, go south on Main Street (WI 89) for one-half block, then straight (south) on County Road A as WI 89 curves left. Continue straight (south) on Mud Lake Road after one-half block as County Road A curves right, and travel 0.7 mile to the first turn. There you can enter the campground on a special trail, which continues straight (south) for 0.3 mile. The motor vehicle entrance is off of Mud Lake Road, 0.5 mile east of the trail entrance.

Traveling west on the Glacial Drumlin State Trail, you come to one of its show spots at 37.5 miles. Here a quarter-mile-long bridge crosses a narrow neck between upper and lower Rock Lake. The view of the lake is wonderful. To the north the largest part is lined with lake homes. To the south, marshland rings the lake edge. The bridge is well designed for fishing, with side decks that keep anglers away from trail traffic.

West of Rock Lake the trail is sheltered until a tunnel underpass of County Road S at 38.7 miles. Then it is mostly open to the sky and wind until you near London. This can be a difficult stretch when a strong wind is blowing from the southwest, which it often does in the warm weather months. Along the way you'll see a wooden bench and an interpretive sign on the north side of the trail. They invite you to stop for a moment and watch a bison herd that grazes the pastures and hillsides, a scene much as it might have been in presettlement days.

Nearing London, the trail crosses Koshkonong Creek, the first of five crossings on the way to the western trailhead. At 42.5 miles the trail reaches County Road O in London. The only service in this crossroads village is a tavern. For other services you can make a 3.4-mile on-road side trip south to Cambridge. Wisconsin Highway 134 between London and Cambridge has a paved shoulder. Cambridge is a pretty village with several little parks. It has become a center for crafts, notably locally made Early American pottery reproductions. There are several cafes and restaurants and a terrific little bakery that has lunch specials.

Between London and Deerfield you'll pass farm fields that benefit from alluvium, the fertile soil that washed off the glacial ice sheet. At 45.7 miles you enter Deerfield, a little town that is rapidly becoming a bedroom community for nearby Madison. Cuda Cafe, adjacent to the trail, is a very popular place for a break.

The final stretch between Deerfield and Cottage Grove is your opportunity to see more unique glacial features. Here the trail winds between drumlins. These long, narrow, oval hills are oriented northeast-southwest, which is the direction the glacial ice sheet moved. The hills are often wooded sanctuaries for birds and wild critters. Why they formed under the ice is still a mystery.

At 47.3 miles the trail bends to the left around the northern tip of a drumlin, and at 48.2 miles a bend to the right takes the trail between two drumlins.

At 52.4 miles you'll reach the western trailhead at County Road N in Cottage Grove. A commercial complex at the trailhead will soon be offering trail food and bicycle rentals. Most of Cottage Grove's services, other than taverns, are located 0.6 mile north of the trailhead on County Road N near the intersection of County Road BB. The services consist of convenience stores, a cafe, pizza restaurant, and supermarket.

Future plans call for extending the Glacial Drumlin State Trail another 7 miles west to connect with city trails in Monona and Madison and the Military Ridge Trail. When completed, it will create a nearly continuous 110 miles of rail trail between Waukesha and Dodgeville.

11 GLACIAL RIVER TRAIL

The Glacial River Trail has a fascinating prehistoric and historic Native American heritage. There are interesting museums in the pleasant town of Fort Atkinson.

Activities:

Location: Fort Atkinson

Length: 8.5 miles

Surface: Asphalt

Wheelchair access: Yes

Precautions: Crossings at town roads require caution. One stretch is on a lightly traveled town road. Indian Mounds Park is reached via a town road. Currently there are no services available along the route.

Food and facilities: There is water and a small bench and shelter at the Farmco Lane parking area. There are a number of fast-food restaurants and convenience stores along Business Wisconsin Highway 26 and U.S. Highway 12 in Fort Atkinson. The Cafe Carpe in the downtown area is a unique dining spot that often features entertainment by folk musicians. The Fireside on Business WI 26 South is a popular dinner theater with professionally produced musicals. Jones Park in Fort Atkinson offers restroom.

Seasons: Open year-round

Access and parking: From US 12 in downtown Fort Atkinson just north of the river, take North Water Street west 1 block to the municipal building parking lot. The trailhead is at the edge of the lot. If you want to bypass Fort Atkinson and begin at the former trailhead, a second lot is located just south of town. From US 12 in Fort Atkinson, take Janesville Avenue (Business WI 26 South) southwest for 2.0 miles to Farmco Lane and turn right (west). A brown and white sign identifies Farmco Lane as the road to the Glacial River Trail. Go 0.2 mile to the parking area on the right (north).

Rentals: Rock River Canoe Rental, (920) 222–6276, www.rockrivercanoe rental.com

Contact: Jefferson County Parks Department, (920) 674–7260. Fort Atkinson Area Chamber of Commerce, (888) SEE–FORT, www.fortchamber.com.

||||||||||||||||||||||||||||||||||||||||||||||||||||||||||||||||||||||||||||||||||||||||||

General Henry Atkinson and his troops built Fort Koshkonong along the Rock River during the Black Hawk War in July 1832. Congress gave the town the general's name in 1841. But the history of this pleasant riverside community didn't begin with General Atkinson. The area is replete with historic Native American sites. Museums recount their legacy, as well as that of European settlers and the farming methods that made Wisconsin the Dairy State. One of the sites is Indian Mounds Park, a short distance off the trail. There you'll see distinctive animal-shaped effigy mounds and walk a section of ancient Native American trail.

Your plunge into agricultural and Native American history can begin in Fort Atkinson at the Hoard Historical Museum and National Dairy Shrine. This first-rate museum complex at 407 Merchants Avenue (just off of US 12 heading south) is open Tuesday through Sunday during the summer; admission is free. One room is filled with thousands of arrowheads, spear points, and stone tools. Another features the Lincoln Era Library and exhibit, which highlights Lincoln's connection with the area during the Black Hawk War in 1832 and on through his presidency. The National Dairy Shrine showcases the story of dairy farming in Wisconsin, America's Dairyland.

Park in the municipal building parking lot on North Water Street, just north of the Rock River. The trail begins heading south here through downtown Fort Atkinson. You will cross a bridge over the river to find Bicentennial Park on your right, where you can see two statues of Native Americans gazing across the waters. They are part of the town's River Walk development. The area was prized by natives for thousands of years. Evidence of three of the nation's most significant mound-building cultures—Hopewell, Mississippian and Effigy—are found in the area. On Riverside Drive, 7 blocks west of Main Street, you'll find the only remaining intaglio Effigy mound. Mound construction sometimes began with an animal-shaped depression. The process of creating the effigy, a panther in this case, was long, and involved numerous ceremonies.

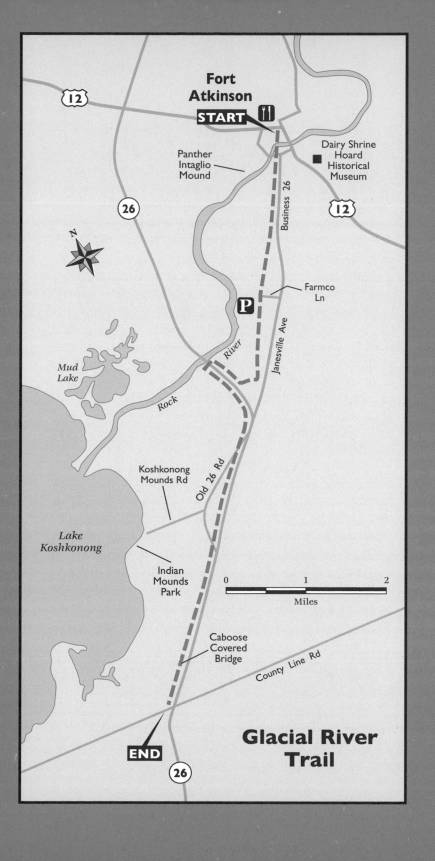

Glacial River Trail

Effigy Mounds Are Unique and Mysterious

When Europeans arrived in southern Wisconsin, they couldn't help but notice distinctive animal-shaped earthen mounds that rose to 3 or 4 feet in height and were typically 75 to 200 feet long. The mounds numbered in the thousands and were often accompanied by conical and linear mounds. Most were located near rivers or lakes. The animal shapes included easily identifiable birds such as swallows, eagles, and geese; mammals such as bear and deer; and puzzling, possibly mythical creatures, like turtles and panthers with extremely long tails.

The mounds were obviously ancient; some had large trees growing out of them. Effigy mounds were found only in the southern half of Wisconsin and narrow bordering areas of Minnesota, Iowa, and Illinois. Area natives had no knowledge of their significance. Many mounds were quickly plowed under by pioneers. Some early scientists surveyed them and conjectured they may have been constructed by some lost race.

As archaeological methods improved, the lost race theory was discarded, but very little was learned about the Effigy Mound culture. When the mounds were used as graves, very few goods were placed with the bodies. The Effigy people must have been seminomadic, because no villages have been found. In the 1980s, scientists knew little more about the mound builders than they did 150 years earlier.

All that has changed. The discovery of a petroglyph carved on a rock shelter wall and a distinctive offering in the shelter floor have tied the Effigy culture to Wisconsin's native Ho Chunk (Winnebago). The carving was clearly of the mythical Ho Chunk trickster Red Horn, and the offering was definitely Effigy culture. Tying the mounds to the Ho Chunk belief in a conflict between an underworld of water spirits and an upper world of spirits of the air begins to explain the positioning of the mounds.

The unique culture flourished over a much narrower time than previously thought, around A.D. 800 to 1100, a time of transition from hunter-gatherer to agricultural societies. By the time Europeans arrived, the mound-building tradition that brought people together to construct these fascinating figures was long forgotten.

Cross Business WI 26 at 0.2 mile, where you'll pass the Rotary Depot Shelter. At 0.4 mile you might check out the exceptional bistro on the left, Everybody's Café & Market. Restrooms are available at Jones Park on your right just past here. At 2.3 miles, traveling southwest from the former trail-head on Farmco Lane, the trail is quiet and wooded. At 3.3 miles the trail intersects Groeler Road. The route is well marked with green and white bicycle silhouette signs. At this point you'll turn right (north) on lightly traveled Groeler Road, heading downhill 0.7 mile to a T intersection with an unmarked town road that passes under the WI 26 bridge along the Rock River. This is a good spot to pause for a look at the Rock, once a major river highway for the Native Americans. Turn left (south) at 4.1 miles, immediately after passing under the bridge, onto Schwemmer Lane, another quiet, dead-end town road.

At 4.6 miles the off-road Glacial River Trail resumes splitting off to the south as Schwemmer Lane turns west. The trail is not on the railroad grade at this point. It rolls gently downhill between farm fields before joining an unnamed town road at 5.2 miles for another short on-road section. At 5.5 miles the road connects with Old 26 Road. At this point the route jogs left (east) a few feet to join the railroad grade, where the paved off-road trail resumes heading southwest. This is also the point where you could take a side trip to Indian Mounds Park by turning right (west) on Old 26 Road, following it for 1.0 mile to Koshkonong Mounds Road, which goes another 1.0 mile west to the park. There, several turtle- and bird-shaped Effigy mounds are preserved, along with a section of Indian trail you can still follow.

A fine day for a family outing on the Glacial River Trail.

Continuing southwest on the Glacial River Trail, you travel through patches of woods and open areas. The trail is close to WI 26 in this section, and vehicles are often visible. At 8.0 miles you come to a covered bridge made and painted in the fashion of a railroad caboose. Local people volunteered to build the structure using wood salvaged from a nearby barn. At 8.5 miles the trail reaches the Jefferson-Rock County line, the present terminus.

12 GREAT RIVER STATE TRAIL

A beautiful collection of rivers great and small, a unique Mississippi River town, and three vast wildlife refuges are encountered along this trail. Near Perrot State Park, one of Wisconsin's most beautiful parks, this is the westernmost link in a nearly continuous 100-mile rail trail system.

Activities:

Note: The trail section in the Trempealeau National Wildlife Refuge is not open for snowmobiling, and no special grooming is done for skiing. Extensive groomed cross-country ski trails are located in Perrot State Park.

Location: Medary to Marshland

Length: 24.4 miles

Surface: Crushed limestone with wood-planked bridges

Wheelchair access: Yes

Precautions: In Onalaska, 0.4 mile of on-street route, including a crossing of Wisconsin Highway 35 at a traffic light, must be traveled to connect the Great River State Trail Visitor Center with the northern part of the trail. Few services are available between Onalaska and Trempealeau, none between Trempealeau and Marshland. In the Trempealeau National Wildlife Refuge, the trail is on gravel roads, 3.5 miles of which may be shared with motor vehicles. Wisconsin State Trails have a carry-in/carry-out policy. Make provisions for carrying out any refuse. No trash receptacles are provided on-trail. The Wisconsin State Trail Pass is required for bicyclists age sixteen and older ($4.00 daily or $20.00 annually). The trail pass also covers usage such as cross-country skiing, horseback riding, and bicycling on state mountain bike trails and other rail trails. Passes can be purchased at Great River State Trail Visitor Center in Onalaska, Onalaska Pro Sports, Trempealeau Hotel, Perrot State Park, at many local businesses, and at self-pay stations at trail parking lots. In winter you must have a Wisconsin snowmobile registration or nonresident trail use sticker.

Food and facilities: Numerous motels, restaurants, and fast-food places are conveniently located in La Crosse just south of the WI 35 exit on Interstate

90. Restaurants and convenience stores are near the trail in Onalaska. There is a tavern in Midway. A restaurant and a cafe are in Trempealeau. A supper club restaurant is near the trailhead in Marshland. Flush toilets and water are at the Medary trailhead parking lot, Great River State Trail Visitor Center in Onalaska, and Perrot State Park. Porta-type toilets are at the trail parking lot in Midway, at the Lyle's Landing parking lot, and at the trail crossing of WI 35 in Trempealeau.

Seasons: Open year-round

Access and parking: To start in Onalaska at the Great River State Trail Visitor Center, exit I–90 at the WI 35 north exit. Go 0.6 mile north on WI 35 (Second Avenue North) and turn right (east) on Oak Forest Drive at the Kwik Trip convenience store. After a half block, follow Oak Forest Drive to the right and park at the Great River State Trail Visitor Center. To start in Trempealeau, park at the WI 35 trail crossing parking lot. To start at the northern end, turn right (south) on the unpaved Marshland Access road immediately east of the railroad track crossing and the WI 35/County Road P junction at Marshland.

Rentals: Blue Heron Bicycle Works, Onalaska, (608) 783–7433. Speed's Bike Shop, Sparta, (608) 269–2315.

Contact: La Crosse Area Convention and Visitors Bureau, (800) 658–9424, www.explorelacrosse.com. La Crosse River State Trail Inc., Sparta Chamber of Commerce (608) 269–4123, www.lacrosseriverstatetrail.org. Onalaska Center for Commerce and Tourism, (800) 873–1901 or (608) 781–9570, www.discoveronalaska.com.

||||||||||||||||||||||||||||||||||||||||||||||||||||||||||||||||||||||||||||||||||

The Mississippi is much more than a great avenue of river commerce and pleasure boating. North America's longest river is lined with emerald green islands and lily pad–filled backwater sloughs that are havens for graceful herons, energetic muskrats, and lurking fish. Along the Great River State Trail, these beautiful features are protected as the Trempealeau National Wildlife Refuge, Van Loon State Wildlife Refuge, and the Upper

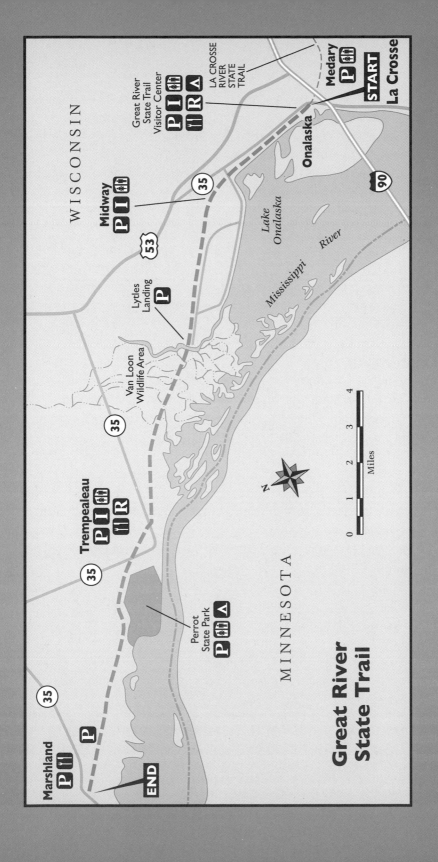

Great River State Trail

Mississippi River Wildlife and Fish Refuge. These refuges are essential links in the Mississippi flyway, the great spring and fall migratory corridor for millions of birds. On just one fall day, more than 50,000 ducks were spotted on the waters of Lake Onalaska.

Once the route of the Chicago and Northwestern Railroad, the Great River State Trail is now an avenue of adventure for self-propelled travelers wishing to explore this wild river world. The fascination of the Mississippi is just part of this experience. Smaller streams and rivers are equally interesting. The trail crosses ten streams along its length. En route, the little town of Trempealeau and Perrot State Park are great places to spend a few hours, an evening, or a weekend.

The Great River State Trail Visitor Center is a nice facility that gives the trail a first-rate trailhead. The trail continues 1.9 miles to the southeast of the visitor center to the junction with the La Crosse River State Trail at Medary, but there is nothing at this point other than parking, water, and restrooms. It does make an excellent connection for people going to the La Crosse River State Trail, which connects to two other state trails, forming a nearly continuous 100-mile rail trail system. Underpasses of busy highways and an overpass bridge across an active rail line between the visitor center and the La Crosse River State Trail make the trip seamless.

If you begin and end your trip in Onalaska, there is a restaurant to keep in mind for dinner on your return. Just a few blocks north of the Great River State Trail Visitor Center on WI 35 (Second Avenue North) at the corner of Main Street is Traditions, which features gourmet cuisine in the unusual setting of the old Onalaska State Bank building. It's a casual setting, but reservations are recommended.

Traveling north from the Great River State Trail Visitor Center (mileage notes are from the visitor center, not the Medary trailhead), you need to follow a well-signed on-street route (green and white signs) for several blocks. Go west on Oak Forest Drive for 1 block to Second Avenue South (WI 35) and cross with the traffic light. Go straight (west) for one-half block. At Court Street, an alley in the middle of the block, turn right (north) and follow it for several blocks to where it rejoins the rail bed trail.

Your best on-trail views of the Mississippi Valley come during the first few miles of travel north from Onalaska. Here the railroad grade makes a gradual descent from the elevated river terrace, where the town is located,

A long iron trestle crosses the Black River.

down to the low floodplain. Occasional breaks in the trailside trees and brush bring glimpses of the river bluffs on the Minnesota shore. The vast expanse of river along this section is called Lake Onalaska.

At 3.2 miles the trail enters the little village of Midway, a barely noticeable cluster of houses. The only service is a tavern. The trail crosses Halfway Creek at 4.1 miles, then travels over a lowland floodplain called Brice Prairie. You won't notice much of it because the trail is tree-sheltered along this stretch.

Leaving the floodplain behind, you enter one of the trail's showplaces. At 7.3 miles you pass the Lyle's Landing trail access point and head into the delta of the Black River. The delta is a maze of streams and sloughs. You will cross five major bridges in 2.5 miles, beginning at 7.8 miles with an impressive 287-foot-long stressed iron trestle over the Black River. The Black River delta and backwaters are part of the Van Loon State Wildlife Refuge. The sloughs (pronounced *slooz*) are great places for spotting a great blue heron stalking fish in the shallow pools, and deer are often seen even in midday.

At 14.3 miles you come to the trail crossing of WI 35 (Third Street) in Trempealeau *(TREMP-ah-low)*. Northwest of this crossing, the trail passes through a residential part of town. To get to the downtown, notably the not-to-be-missed Trempealeau Hotel, turn left (west) on Third Street and go 0.7 mile to Main Street. Turn right (south) on Main Street and go a block and a half to the hotel.

The Trempealeau Hotel is in a quaint old false-front building near the edge of the Burlington Northern rail line and the Mississippi shore. There are rooms for rent upstairs (with a shared bath), so it is still really a hotel. Downstairs space is devoted to a restaurant and an ornate bar. The walls are covered with photos from the town's past, and the menu features something for everyone, including, of all things, a walnut burger.

Just a half block downhill from the hotel, First Street goes to the west. It is one of the on-road routes to Perrot *(PAIR-oh)* State Park. Your other options for accessing the park include the following: Rejoin the Great River State Trail either by backtracking or by going north on Main Street for 0.6 mile to the trail crossing point and turning left (northwest) onto the trail. After 1.8 miles (or at 17.1 on-trail miles from the Great River State Trail Visitor Center), the trail crosses Lehman Road. At this point you can turn left (south) and make an immediate right turn (west) onto the Perrot State Park entrance road. Alternately, you could continue west on the trail for 0.6 mile (17.7 on-trail miles) to a short spur trail that goes south into the park campground.

Perrot State Park encompasses five towering 400-foot-high bluffs that face the Mississippi. Hiking and mountain bike trails can take you up top for some incomparable views. A favorite hike is up to Brady's Bluff, where you can see the Trempealeau National Wildlife Refuge and Trempealeau Mountain to the west. This unique isolated hill was a river landmark for thousands of years for numerous traders, from the extensive Native American Hopewell culture to the early French explorers. Nicholas Perrot wintered in the park in 1685. The park's nature center is a great place to learn about the geological and human history of the area.

The westernmost stretch of the Great River State Trail takes you into the Trempealeau National Wildlife Refuge for a closer look. At 20.0 miles the trail leaves the rail bed at the Refuge Road access point and follows gravel refuge roads. Isolated by three railroad grades, the 5,700-acre refuge is a tranquil breeding ground for myriad waterfowl.

At 22.5 miles you reach the northern end of the Great River State Trail at the Marshland Access parking lot.

13 LA CROSSE RIVER STATE TRAIL

Set in a quiet rural area, the La Crosse River State Trail passes through pleasant small towns. It connects to the Great River State Trail and the Elroy-Sparta State Trail.

Activities:

Location: Sparta to Medary

Length: 21.5 miles

Surface: Crushed limestone with wood-planked bridges

Wheelchair access: Yes

Precautions: There are many open sections; sunblock is recommended. The Wisconsin State Trail Pass is required for bicyclists age sixteen and older ($4.00 daily or $20.00 annually). The trail pass also covers usage such as cross-country skiing, horseback riding, and bicycling on state mountain bike trails and other rail trails. Passes can be purchased at the Sparta Depot, at many area businesses, and at self-pay stations at trail parking lots. In winter you must have a Wisconsin snowmobile registration or nonresident trail use sticker.

Food and facilities: Numerous restaurants and fast-food places are located in La Crosse just south of the Wisconsin Highway 35 and Wisconsin Highway 16 exits from Interstate 90. Restaurants and convenience stores are near the trail in Onalaska, 1.9 miles north of Medary on the Great River State Trail. Numerous restaurants and fast-food places are near the trailhead in Sparta. Cafes and groceries are in West Salem and Bangor. Flush toilets and water are at the Sparta Depot, Bangor Village Park, Veterans Park, and the Medary trailhead. Shuttle service is offered by Speed's Bicycle Sales and Service in Sparta. Speed's also offers a wide variety of on-trail and on-road bicycle tours.

Seasons: Open year-round

Access and parking: From the I–90 Wisconsin Highway 27/Sparta exit, travel north for 0.2 mile and turn right (east) on Avon Road. Go 0.7 mile to

South Water Street and turn left (north). Go 0.3 mile to Milwaukee Street and park at the Sparta Depot at 111 Milwaukee Street and South Water Street. For the western trailhead at Medary, take the I–90 U.S. Highway 53 exit and travel south for 0.7 mile, turn right (south) on WI Highway 16, and travel 0.7 mile to County Road B. Turn left (east) and travel 0.4 mile to the La Crosse River State Trail trailhead parking lot.

Rentals: Speed's Bicycle Sales and Service, Sparta, (608) 269–2315.

Contact: Sparta Area Chamber of Commerce, (608) 269–4123, www.sparta wisconsin.org. La Crosse Area Convention and Visitors Bureau, (800) 658–9424 or (608) 782–2364, www.explorelacrosse.com.

|||||||||||||||||||||||||||||||||||||||||||||||||||||||||||||||||||||||||||||||||||||||

When French fur traders visited the broad floodplain along the Mississippi River, they witnessed a uniquely American game. The Native Americans who had gathered for the trading rendezvous formed two teams equipped with scooplike rackets. The object was to get a ball through opposing goals. Hundreds might be on a single team, and the goals were often a mile apart. The traders called this unforgettable game *la crosse.*

The city, river, and trail that bear the name today are well worth a visit. La Crosse itself is a pleasant small city with museums, parks, and, of course, a wonderful location on the mighty Mississippi. For a great view of the city and river from 600 feet up, make a side trip to the park at the top of Grandad Bluff. Or get close to the water with an excursion on the stern-wheel riverboat the *La Crosse Queen.*

The La Crosse River State Trail once carried the Chicago and Northwestern Railroad. In 1948 Harry Truman traveled the line in his famous "whistle-stop" presidential campaign. He got out the rural vote, and the day after the election a smiling Truman held up a copy of the *Chicago Tribune* with the erroneous headline "Dewey Beats Truman." Just goes to show that election-year media debacles are nothing new.

An exciting aspect of the La Crosse River State Trail is that it closely parallels the active Chicago, Milwaukee, St. Paul & Pacific Railroad line.

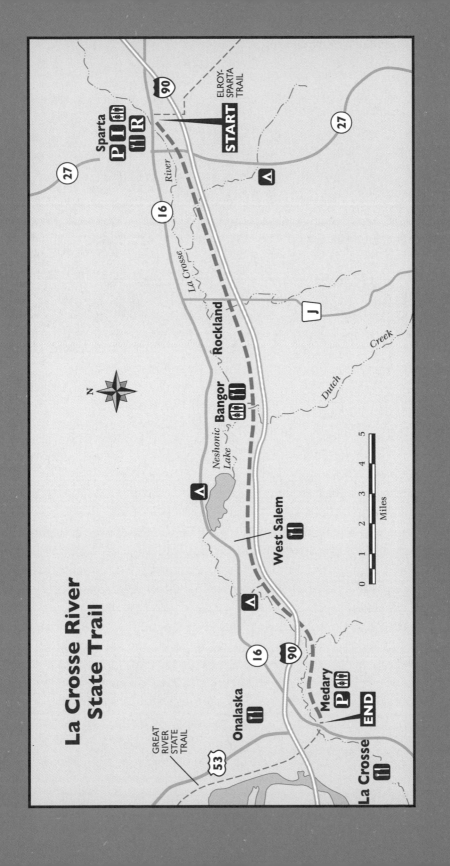

La Crosse River State Trail

START

END

Sparta
P 🚻 🍴 R

27

90

ELROY-
SPARTA
TRAIL

27

16

River

La Crosse

J

Creek

Dutch

Rockland

Bangor
🍴 🚻

Neshonic
Lake

West Salem
🍴

N

5
4
3
Miles
2
1
0

16

90

Medary
P 🚻

Onalaska
🍴

GREAT
RIVER
STATE
TRAIL

53

La Crosse
🍴

A quiet "tunnel through the trees" along the La Crosse River State Trail.

The "Milwaukee Road" is a prosperous line that hauls freight to and from the Twin Cities of Minnesota and beyond. Riding or walking along as a freight train rolls by in the same direction gives a strange illusion of going backward. Backward or forward, you can expect a friendly wave from the train engineers.

The best starting point for the La Crosse River State Trail is at the trail headquarters at the Sparta Depot. The depot is also the location of the Sparta Tourism Bureau, a clearinghouse for all sorts of information on area services and events. For more than a decade, Sparta has promoted itself as the "Bicycle Capital of America," and the town does a great job of welcoming bicycling visitors. At a town park a few blocks north of the depot is a "must do" photo opportunity. A sculpture of the "world's largest bicycle" makes a great background for a snapshot of your visit.

Another unique bicycle attraction is located downtown. The Deke Slayton Memorial Space and Bike Museum honors hometown astronaut Deke Slayton and displays a collection of unique bicycles. You'll see everything from iron-wheeled bone shakers to the no-nonsense mountain bike local rider Olga McNulty rode to win Alaska's on-snow Iditabike race.

Traveling west from the Sparta Depot, the trail crosses County Road J at 6.0 miles, just south of Rockland. You can't miss the tiny village, thanks to the water tower you've likely seen miles in advance. To get into town, turn right (north) and travel 0.3 mile on County Road J, where you'll find Mike's Mini Mart, a good place for snacks and sandwiches.

At 9.3 miles the trail crosses County Road B on the outskirts of Bangor. Just north of the crossing, County Road B turns to parallel the trail and becomes Commercial Street, Bangor's main street. Heading west along the trail, a spur trail to the north at 9.9 miles passes through a little tunnel under the Milwaukee Road line. The spur trail takes you to pleasant Village Park with its shaded picnic area and playground.

Passing West Salem, the trail crosses Leonard Street, West Salem's main street, at 14.3 miles. Here you'll find a couple of places to stop for a bite to eat. If you are interested in historic nineteenth-century architecture, a trip around West Salem will show you two octagon houses and other distinctive buildings, including the home of Hamlin Garland, a Pulitzer Prize–winning author who was born in West Salem in 1860.

At 15.8 miles a spur trail to the north leads 0.3 mile to Veterans Park, a public campground with a store, shelter, and playgrounds. At 21.4 miles the La Crosse River State Trail meets the Great River State Trail at an overpass bridge that crosses the Milwaukee Road line to the north. At 21.5 miles you arrive at the Medary trailhead.

14 MILITARY RIDGE STATE TRAIL

The Military Ridge State Trail affords beautiful views from the ridgetop, passes through interesting trail towns, and provides access to Blue Mound State Park and Governor Dodge State Park.

Activities:

Note: There is no special grooming for skiing, but groomed trails are in Blue Mound State Park and Governor Dodge State Park.

Location: Madison to Dodgeville

Length: 42.2 miles

Surface: Crushed limestone with wood-planked bridges; some seal-coated limestone sections between Ridgeway and Dodgeville and on spur trails into the state parks

Wheelchair access: Yes

Precautions: The trail leaves the rail bed and follows the natural rolling terrain on an seal-coated limestone section between Ridgeway and Dodgeville. Spur trails into Blue Mound State Park and Governor Dodge State Park are very steep. The trail is mostly open, with occasional shaded stretches. The use of sunblock is advised. Wisconsin State Trails have a carry-in/carry-out policy. Make provisions for carrying out any refuse. No trash receptacles are provided on-trail. The Wisconsin State Trail Pass is required for bicyclists age sixteen and older ($4.00 daily or $20.00 annually). The trail pass also covers usage such as cross-country skiing, horseback riding, and bicycling on state mountain bike trails and other rail trails. Passes can be purchased at Atkins Verona Bicycle Shoppe near Verona, the Barneveld State Bank, and at self-pay stations at all Military Ridge State Trail parking areas. In winter you must have a Wisconsin snowmobile registration or nonresident trail use sticker.

Food and facilities: There are no services at or near the trailhead. Restaurants and fast-food places are located in Verona along Business U.S. Highway 18/151. There is a tavern that serves some food in Riley. Mt. Horeb has several restaurants a half block north of the trail. There is a cafe away from the trail in Barneveld. Dodgeville has several restaurants and fast-food places near the trailhead. There are taverns in all trail towns except Klevenville. There is a swimming pool in Blue Mound State Park. Swimming beaches are at Stewart County Park in Mt. Horeb and at Governor Dodge State Park. Playgrounds are at Grundahl Park in Mt. Horeb, Blue Mounds Village Park, Memorial Park in Barneveld, and the Ridgeway Village Park. Flush toilets and water are at Grundahl Park in Mt. Horeb, Blue Mounds Village Park, Blue Mound State Park, Memorial Park in Barneveld, and Governor Dodge State Park. Pit toilets are at the village park in Ridgeway.

Seasons: Open year-round

Access and parking: Currently the trailhead is at the intersection of County Road PD/McKee Road and Verona Road/US 18/151 in Madison, but plans are to connect it in the near future to the Capital City State Trail and Southwest Path as part of the new and developing Badger State Trail. To get here from the Capital City State Trail, follow the frontage road southwest 0.7 mile. There is no parking here. For the parking area near Verona, different directions apply if you are traveling east or west. Coming from the east on US 18/151, exit at the Verona Business US 18/151 interchange and continue west to Old PB Road. Turn left (south) on Old PB Road and immediately turn right (west) into the Military Ridge State Trail parking area. Coming from the west on US 18/151, exit at the County Road MV/Old PB Road exit and turn left (north) on Old PB Road. Continue north for 1.0 mile and turn left (west) into the Military Ridge State Trail parking area. For the western trailhead at Dodgeville, turn north at the intersection of US 18/151 and Wisconsin Highway 23 and immediately turn right (east) into the Military Ridge State Trail parking area.

Rentals: Atkins Verona Bicycle Shoppe, (608) 845–6644.

Contact: Dodgeville Revitalization Chamber, Tourist Information, (608) 935–5993, www.dodgeville.com. Military Ridge State Trail, (608) 437–7393. Mt. Horeb Area Chamber of Commerce, (608) 437–5914 or (888) 765–5929, www.trollway.com. Wisconsin Department of Natural Resources, (608) 266–2181, www.dnr.state.wi.us.

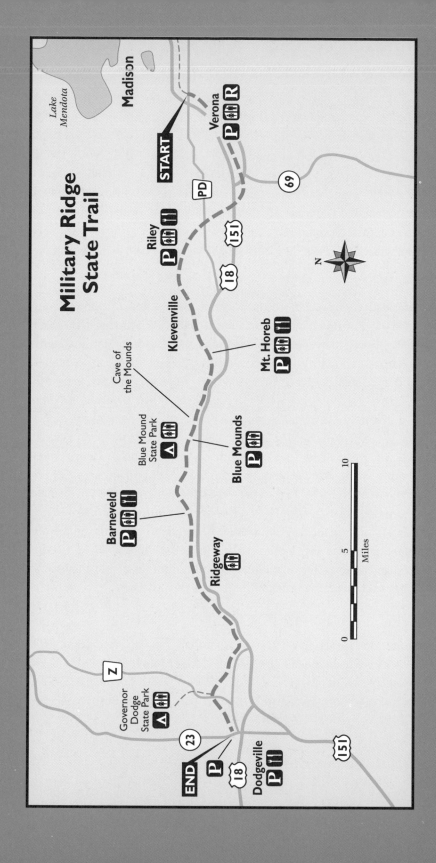

Military Ridge State Trail

If nothing else, you'll remember the view from the Military Ridge. To the north the land drops away steeply, fragmenting into deep, twisting, wooded valleys. Looking south, the terrain slopes more gently. Narrow bands of different crops wrap around the contours of the side valleys, creating fascinating patterns. A trip on the ridge is a passage by some of the most beautiful scenes nature and farming can create.

Whether you travel from the east or west end, the flat-topped, wooded silhouette of Blue Mound dominates the horizon. The highest point in southern Wisconsin, this singular hill rises more than 500 feet above the trail. A spur trail allows you to enter the park that protects this landmark.

Trail towns vary greatly. Verona is a sprawling bedroom community that the trail merely skirts on its south edge. Riley has the Riley Tavern, and Klevenville is just a cluster of houses. Blue Mounds barely warrants a nod. Barneveld and Ridgeway are simply a few buildings and businesses. The trailhead at Dodgeville is next to an expanding commercial district just north of a fascinating early-nineteenth-century downtown.

The history of Military Ridge goes back before the days of the Chicago and Northwestern Railroad, the flood of settlers heading west, or the American soldiers traveling between distant frontier forts. For thousands of years a Native American trail followed the ridge, offering views of herds of buffalo on vast expanses of tall prairie grass that rolled like ocean waves in the wind. And always, the outline of Blue Mound beckoned them. It was a sacred place where they gathered chert, a flintlike rock, to make tools and projectile points.

The Military Ridge State Trail has been extended 2.9 miles to the east to connect, after a 0.6 mile on-street link, with the Nine Springs E-Way/Capital City Trail and the Southwest Path, which in turn will allow you to hike or ride all the way to downtown Madison. At some future time the Capital City Trail will be linked to the Glacial Drumlin State Trail, making a continuous 110-mile trail system.

The Verona trailhead is not on the ridge. You'll begin your trip in the lowland. Gently rolling farmland and fields—fields that seem to grow new barnlike suburban houses these days—make up the scenery, and trailside brush gives some sense of isolation. At 1.1 miles the trail crosses Wisconsin Highway 69 as it skirts the south edge of Verona. There are no services near the trail, but WI 69 is a town street here, and signs show the way to downtown. This is the last grade-level crossing of a significant highway along the trail. All others will be made on overpass bridges or underpasses.

West of Verona, the Military Ridge looms ahead. It seems the trail does all it can to put off the climb as long as possible as it makes a wide swing to the north. At 7.1 miles the trail passes Riley, my favorite starting point, home to the Riley Tavern and a smattering of houses. Riley is off the beaten path, a great place to sit on the front porch and watch trail traffic go by. The tavern has become a gathering point for bluegrass musicians who often gather to pick and sing, and the Sunday morning pancakes are quite popular.

Leaving Riley, the trail begins toying with the hills. On the way to Klevenville, it goes through a deep cut in the sandstone along the edge of one hill. This is a nicely shaded section where you can feel the cool of the rock on a hot day. Out in the open again, at 9.6 miles, the trail passes through Klevenville, which only amounts to a few scattered houses these days. At 9.9 miles the climb up to the Military Ridge begins. When you reach Mt. Horeb just over 3 miles away, you'll be 250 feet higher. You won't notice the grade too much, but it will slow you, giving you more time to enjoy this intimate section of trail. Mature maples, oaks, and aspens make it one of the shadiest stretches. There are few road crossings except for the occasional gravel farm field access road.

Your entry into Mt. Horeb is preceded by crossing the high railroad bridge over Business US 18/151. In town the trail parallels Main Street, just 1 block to the south. At 13.1 miles you cross Second Street, which is your best access to the Main Street shops, most notably Schubert's restaurant and bakery, where the macaroons are heavenly. Beer connoisseurs may want to check out the nearby brew pub, The Grumpy Troll.

Traveling west from Mt. Horeb, you know you're on top of the ridge. The land falls away on both sides, and there is an open, top-of-the-world feeling. Ahead is the beautiful shape of Blue Mound, so named because it has a bluish hue when seen from far away. The closer you get the greener it gets. On the way, a tunnel takes you under County Road ID.

There is a wonderful attraction near the village of Blue Mounds. Cave of the Mounds has fascinated visitors since its discovery more than sixty years ago. The temperature is a constant 50 degrees in this marvelous

The Military Ridge State Trail skirts the edge of Blue Mound State Park.

world of subterranean pools and glistening, icicle-like stalactites. The cave is open daily for one-hour guided tours. To get there from the trail, stop at the little wayside picnic area on the south side of the trail 0.1 mile west of the underpass tunnel. Go south around the wayside gate onto County Road ID and turn left (east). Go east 0.1 mile to Cave of the Mounds Road, turn left (northwest), and continue 0.3 mile to the Cave of the Mounds parking area.

Before reaching Blue Mound, you must go through the village of Blue Mounds, one of the oldest towns in the state. The village's name is plural because there is actually a second, lower mound mainly visible from the north.

During the Black Hawk War, in the summer of 1832, miners and settlers fled to a small fort just north of the trail. After two weeks inside the fort, with no sign of any Native Americans, two men went out to cut wood. As they reached the edge of the forest, they were instantly ambushed and killed.

Blue Mound is much more tranquil these days. You won't see much of the tiny town. The trail is a few blocks away from Main Street, where all you'll find is a tavern. At 18.2 miles you reach a little town park with a playground and ball field at the crossing of Mound Road. A concession stand operates there when a ball game is going on.

Continuing west, the trail skirts the southern slope of Blue Mound. Here you enter a beautifully sheltered 2-mile trail section, a tunnel through the thick maples and oaks. At 18.9 miles a spur trail goes north into Blue Mound State Park. A side trip into the park is well worth the effort—and it will take effort. The spur trail is very steep. You'll climb 160 feet in 0.3 mile before reaching the campground drive. Blessedly, the spur trail is asphalt. At the campground, turn right (northeast) and follow the drive for 0.3 mile to a T intersection with the park entrance road. Turn left (northwest) and go 0.4 mile to the top of the mound. This is another extremely steep climb, covering more than 200 feet of elevation.

Along the way you'll pass the turn to the park's swimming pool. This may be as far as you want to go on a hot day. If you make it to the top, there are east and west observation towers. On a clear day you can see the State Capitol, 40 miles away. On any day, the view of the ridge and valleys is spectacular.

Going west on the Military Ridge State Trail, you come to a gap in the woods on the south side of the trail at 20.5 miles. A wooden bench at the top of the grade cut is a wonderful rest stop with a great view of ribbons of different crops curving along the contours of the land.

At 20.8 miles the trail emerges from the woods into an open sumac-sided channel. In this trough, I once found myself riding along with a fluttering group of monarch butterflies, propelled along at my speed by the ridge top wind. Ahead stands the Barneveld water tower, one of the structures that survived when a tornado obliterated parts of the town on a June night in 1984. The storm was so fierce it actually bent the tower. In town, at 22.1 miles, is pleasant little Memorial Park, dedicated to the memory of the storm's victims.

At 27.3 miles the trail passes the north side of Ridgeway, a little village that seems forgotten since the rerouting of US 18/151 to the south. The little village park is the only notable thing in town.

About 5 miles farther west, the trail swings to the northwest. At 34.3 miles it crosses County Road Z. At this point you can follow a 1.4-mile-long asphalt spur trail that runs north along County Road Z and then cuts northwest into Governor Dodge State Park. In a way, the park is the mirror image of Blue Mound. Its points of interest—towering rock formations and a nice swimming beach—are at the bottom of a steep valley. That means it is easy to get into and a hard climb getting out.

Back on Military Ridge State Trail, the rail bed makes a 120-degree bend to the southwest as it heads to Dodgeville. At 39.3 miles you'll reach the western trailhead at WI 23. At this point you are just 0.2 mile north of the town's strip of modern commerce, which notably includes a classic A&W Root Beer stand. The real classic part of Dodgeville is 1.0 mile south of the trailhead. There you'll find Iowa Street, the town's main street, and blocks of nineteenth-century brick and stone storefront buildings. In their midst is the impressive 1859 Greek Revival Iowa County Courthouse. They built things to last in those days.

15 OAKLEAF TRAIL

A surprisingly secluded trail in the midst of Milwaukee, the Oakleaf Trail has great views of Lake Michigan plus all the services and attractions a city like Milwaukee can offer.

Activities:

Location: Milwaukee

Length: 5.5 miles (this trail is part of a much larger system of nearly 100 miles of streets, parkway drives, and other off-road sections that make a citywide loop)

Surface: Asphalt

Wheelchair access: Yes

Precautions: Despite the entirely urban route of the trail, access to services is minimal.

Food and facilities: The Miller Brewing Company Pavilion and Coast Restaurant are located on the top level of O'Donnell Park. Near the Capitol Drive overpass you can exit the trail into a restaurant parking lot. Another restaurant is nearby.

Seasons: Open year-round

Access and parking: For the southern trailhead, from Interstate 794 eastbound, take the Jackson/Van Buren exit. Turn left (north) on Van Buren Street and travel 2 blocks to Michigan Avenue. Turn right (east) and travel 2 blocks to the O'Donnell Park lower-level parking lot entrance on the north side of the avenue. For the northern trailhead, from Interstate 43, exit at Capitol Drive. Travel east 1.5 miles to Estabrook Parkway. Turn left (north), travel 0.1 mile, and turn right (east) into the Kilbourntown House parking lot.

Rentals: Bicycle and in-line skate rentals are available from Milwaukee Bike and Skate Rental in Veterans Park, (414) 273–1343.

A rock climber practices on a wall along the Oakleaf Trail.

Contact: Milwaukee County Parks, (414) 257–7275. Greater Milwaukee Convention and Visitors Bureau, (800) 231–0903. Betty Brinn Children's Museum, (414) 390–5437.

The Chicago and Northwestern Railroad once ran along the rail bed that now carries the Oakleaf Trail. Actually, this is just a section of the Oakleaf Trail, which, in its totality, is a near 100-mile system of off-road and

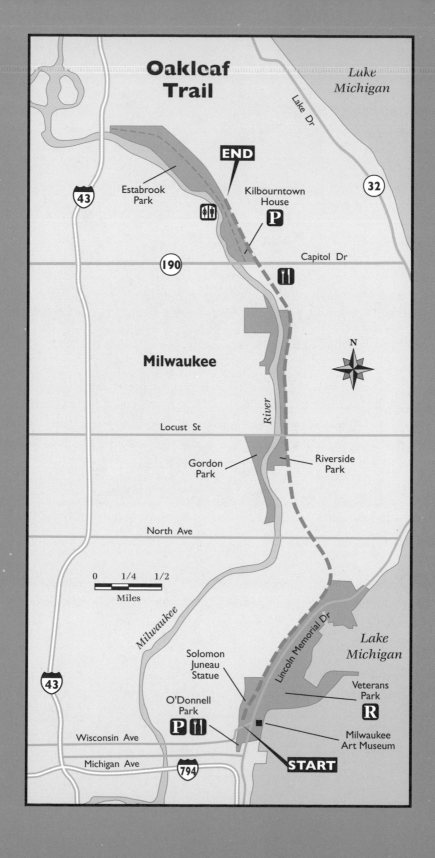

Oakleaf Trail

Lake Michigan

Lake Dr

43

END

Estabrook Park

Kilbourntown House

P

32

190

Capitol Dr

🍴

Milwaukee

N

River

Locust St

Gordon Park

Riverside Park

North Ave

0   1/4   1/2

Miles

Milwaukee

Lincoln Memorial Dr

Solomon Juneau Statue

Lake Michigan

O'Donnell Park

P 🍴

Veterans Park

R

Milwaukee Art Museum

Wisconsin Ave

START

Michigan Ave

794

on-street routes that travels through parkland and circles Milwaukee. This popular section offers a chance to get away from the hustle and bustle and still be close enough to the city's attractions, parks, and restaurants to make a great day of your visit.

The Betty Brinn Children's Museum in O'Donnell Park is always a hit with kids. Along the route is the Milwaukee Art Museum, which displays nearly 20,000 works of art. Great views of Lake Michigan and the Milwaukee River are all part of the experience. Just south of the museum at Pier Wisconsin is Discovery World, where you'll also see the *Dennis Sullivan*, a re-creation of a Great Lakes schooner. The ship makes its home here each summer.

O'Donnell Park is more a building than a park in the conventional sense. On the upper level it houses the Betty Brinn Children's Museum, the Miller Brewing Company Pavilion, and the Coast Restaurant. On the lower level is an indoor parking facility. This is a good starting point for the Oakleaf Trail. Exit through the Michigan Avenue entrance and turn right (west) on the adjacent sidewalk, then turn right (north) at the west end of the building and follow the pedestrian ramp up to the upper level of the park. If you are bicycling, it will be best to walk your bike. Continue north on the sidewalk and at 0.1 mile cross Lincoln Memorial Drive at the traffic light. The Oakleaf Trail begins on the opposite side of Lincoln Memorial Drive.

As you start down a moderately steep hill on the paved trail, you can see the statue of Milwaukee's founder, fur trader Solomon Juneau, up the embankment to the left. At the bottom of the hill at 0.4 mile, you begin traveling on the old railroad grade. You'll have some nice views of Lake Michigan, the lagoon in Veterans Park, and the McKinley Marina along this section. At 1.0 mile there is a traffic light on Lincoln Memorial Drive at Lagoon Drive that provides an opportunity to cross over into Veterans Park.

At 1.5 miles the trail begins to swing away from the lake into a deep grade cut. A spur trail that goes up to Lafayette Place splits off to the right at 1.6 miles. Continuing north on the Oakleaf Trail, you'll travel through four city street underpasses. The sides of the underpasses are built of large quarried limestone blocks. You may see rock climbers practicing on these walls.

The trail has a quiet wooded character hiding the old industrial area you are passing through. At 2.8 miles a spur trail splits off to the right by Riverside High School. It connects with Locust Street. On the west side of the trail is Riverside Park, a wild, abandoned place that has a *Secret Garden* feel. Parks along the river were popular when people boarded excursion boats downtown and traveled upstream for a day of fun. Many of these parks fell into disuse with the coming of the automobile. Recent revitalization and the development of the Riverwalk have brought back their charm and popularity, and boat tours are increasingly popular.

Passing under Locust Street, you begin the most scenic section of the trail. It runs very close to the Milwaukee River here, though about 50 feet above the water level. You'll catch some nice views of the river, especially in the fall and early spring when there are few leaves on the trees.

At 4.5 miles, just before an overpass bridge of Capitol Drive, you can exit the trail into the parking lot of a Bakers Square restaurant. If you follow the Capitol Drive sidewalk to the west, passing under the trail bridge, you'll find the Riverbrook Restaurant and Frozen Custard Stand.

Continuing north on the Oakleaf Trail, at 4.6 miles you'll come to a side trail on the west side that leads to the Kilbourntown House parking lot. Kilbourntown House is the oldest building in Milwaukee. The simple white 1844 Greek Revival house was moved to this spot from its original location not far from your starting point.

You could choose to cross Estabrook Drive opposite the point at which the side trail entered the Kilbourntown House parking lot and ride on a trail winding through Estabrook Park. This is also part of the Oakleaf Trail system. If you follow it north for 0.7 mile, you will come to a modern playground. The park office building across Estabrook Drive has water and flush toilets.

Continuing north on the rail bed portion of the Oakleaf Trail, you arrive at the northern end of the developed portion at 5.5 miles at Wilson Drive and Congress Street.

16 OLD ABE STATE TRAIL

Wonderful views of the broad Chippewa River and woodland scenery permeate the Old Abe Trail. Along the way you'll visit Brunet Island State Park and the interesting city of Chippewa Falls.

Activities:

Location: Cornell to Chippewa Falls

Length: 18.1 miles, including the 1.2-mile link to Brunet Island State Park (5.6 miles of parallel equestrian trail run from Jim Falls to the southern trailhead)

Surface: Asphalt; natural surface for the parallel equestrian trail

Wheelchair access: Yes

Precautions: There are several county road crossings. Take care not to frighten horses on the adjacent riding path. Wisconsin State Trails have a carry-in/carry-out policy. Make provisions for carrying out any refuse. No trash receptacles are provided on-trail. The Wisconsin State Trail Pass is required for bicyclists, equestrians, and in-line skaters age sixteen and older ($4.00 daily or $20.00 annually). The trail pass also covers usage such as cross-country skiing and bicycling on state mountain bike trails and other rail trails. Passes can be purchased at self-pay stations at the southern, Jim Falls, and Cornell trail parking areas, at the Brunet Island State Park office, at the Lake Wissota State Park office, and at some local businesses. In winter you must have a Wisconsin snowmobile registration or nonresident trail use sticker.

Food and facilities: All services are available in Chippewa Falls. There are no facilities at the southern trailhead. Anson Park, near Jim Falls, has a playground, an open shelter, a pop machine, and clean pit toilets. There are a convenience store and a restaurant in Jim Falls. Cornell has a grocery, convenience stores, and several cafes. Brunet Island State Park has an open shelter, a playground, a swimming beach, camping, showers, water, and flush toilets.

Seasons: Open year-round

Access and parking: From the junction of Wisconsin Highway 27 and Wisconsin Highway 64 in Cornell, travel west on WI 64 for 0.2 mile and turn right (north) on Park Road. Travel 1.2 miles to the Brunet Island State Park office and visitor center parking lot. From Wisconsin Highway 178 (East Grand Avenue) and Wisconsin Highway 124 (North High Street) in downtown Chippewa Falls, follow WI 178 northeast 2.6 miles to County Road S. Turn right (east) on County Road S and travel 2.4 miles to 97th Avenue/Elks Club Drive. Turn left (west) and make an immediate right turn (north) into the Old Abe State Trail parking lot. The Jim Falls trail access is located along the east side of County Road S just south of the Cenex convenience store.

Rentals: None

Contact: Chippewa Valley Convention and Visitors Bureau, (888) 523–3866 or (715) 831–2345, www.chippewavalley.net. Wisconsin Department of Natural Resources, (715) 232–1242. Lake Wissota State Park, (715) 382–4574.

|||||||||||||||||||||||||||||||||||||||||||||||||||||||||||||||||||||||||||||||||

There's an interesting story surrounding the trail's name. Old Abe was a bald eagle raised from infancy near Jim Falls. When the Civil War broke out, Old Abe was adopted as the mascot of the Eighth Wisconsin Infantry Regiment. The brave eagle was carried into thirty-nine battles and survived to live to a ripe old age.

There is more to the Old Abe State Trail than just the trail itself. Brunet Island State Park is a gem of a park at the site of Frenchman Jean Brunet's trading post. Miles of nature trails explore the lush island forest. It's a great location to base your trail adventure from. A 1.2-mile paved trail link from the park to the town of Cornell and the Old Abe State Trail makes the experience seamless.

The city of Chippewa Falls is an attraction in itself. It will prove to be more so in the future as links are developed from the current southern trailhead into the city's downtown.

When completed, the trail links will provide trail access to Irvine Park, where a rambunctious herd of buffalo roams, and Jacob Leinenkugel's Brewery. One of Wisconsin's oldest small brewers, "Leinie's" welcomes beer

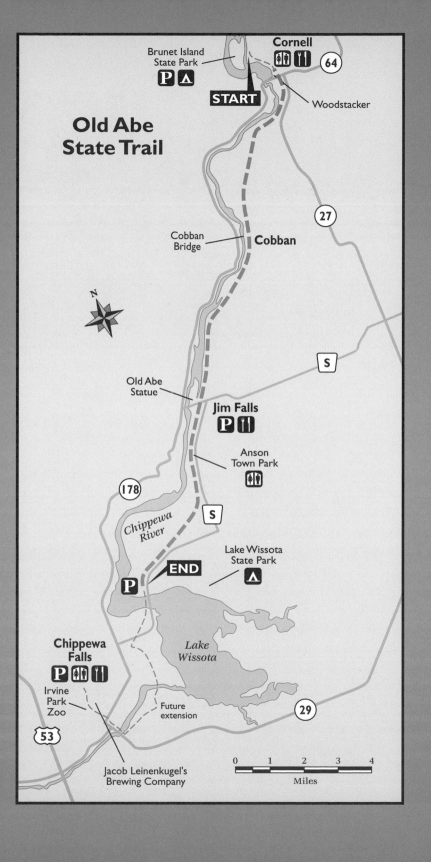

Old Abe State Trail

Cornell

64

Brunet Island State Park

START

Woodstacker

27

Cobban Bridge — **Cobban**

N

S

Old Abe Statue

Jim Falls

Anson Town Park

178

S

Chippewa River

Lake Wissota State Park

END

P

Chippewa Falls

Irvine Park Zoo

53

Future extension

Lake Wissota

29

Jacob Leinenkugel's Brewing Company

0   1   2   3   4
Miles

The "Stacker" rises in the distance near Cornell.

lovers for free tours and sampling daily throughout the summer months. Reservations are recommended; phone (888) LEINIES, www.leinies.com.

Traveling from Brunet Island State Park, you'll follow Park Road from the park office and visitor center back toward the park entrance and pick up the trail link to the Old Abe State Trail on the north side of the road at 0.1 mile. The asphalt-paved trail link does not travel on a railroad bed. It winds through a forest of pine trees until it crosses Park Road at 0.4 mile. From there the trail parallels the road for another half mile, then crosses Park Road again. At 1.0 mile it begins running on the rail bed, and at 1.2 miles the trail officially becomes the Old Abe State Trail at the crossing of Main Street. There are an information board and self-pay station at this point.

Traveling south, you cross a high trestle over WI 64 at 1.3 miles. This is a great spot for a view of the "Stacker," a huge 175-foot-long iron-girder crane left over from the lumbering era. Floating logs down the Chippewa River was the cheapest way of transportation, and Cornell was an ideal spot to stack logs for the pulp mills. At 2.6 miles you'll catch the smell of fresh-cut lumber, like a scent of the lumberjack era. You'll be deep among the maples, oaks, and aspens for the next 4 miles, with plenty of time to think about those bygone days.

At 6.6 miles you'll cross County Road K. Take a look down K to the west to see the amazing narrow, stressed-iron Cobban Bridge. Built in 1908, it is the oldest Pennsylvania Overhead Truss–type bridge in the state. You can get another perspective on the delicate-looking twin-span bridge at 6.9 miles by pausing on the wooden trail bridge for a look back up the river.

Expanses of woods and wonderful stretches of river views will alternate for another 4 miles. The woods are charming with their mix of maple and white paper birch. The river is wide here, backed up by the hydroelectric dam at Jim Falls. At 11.4 miles you'll see the dam up ahead. The Chippewa is a "young" river, still seeking its course since the glacier melted a mere 10,000 years ago. A river like the Chippewa has a steep flow, providing the power to move logs, run sawmills, and generate electricity.

At 12.0 miles the trail crosses County Road S at the north end of the village of Jim Falls. To visit the statue of Old Abe, leave the trail and travel west for 0.2 mile. The statue is at the junction of County Road S and County Road Y (South 138th Avenue). You can get a look at the hydroelectric dam at this spot as well. To return to the trail, either backtrack on County Road S or turn south on County Road Y and travel 0.4 mile to the Old Abe State Trail parking area just south of the Cenex convenience store.

If you forgo the side trip to the Old Abe statue and continue south on the trail, you'll arrive at the trail parking area at 12.5 miles. At 13.6 miles is a short spur trail into Anson Park. The strange-looking dirt area with bleacher seating on each side is for horse pulls. If you are lucky enough to catch one of these tests of strength, you'll be treated to a glimpse of yesteryear. The power of workhorses is just as impressive today as it was then. Across County Road S from the horse pull area, the park stretches down to the banks of the Chippewa—a good spot to take a break in the shade.

At 14.0 miles the trail crosses County Road S in an S curve (which is a safe way of routing the trail so the crossing is at a right angle with good visibility). You'll now ride the most open stretch of the trail. Watch for grazing cattle and horses in the farm fields. At 18.1 miles you arrive at the southern trailhead parking lot.

Future plans are to continue this trail south to connect to the Chippewa River State Trail. You will see that the bridge over the river and into Chippewa Falls just south of the southern trailhead is already completed.

Old Abe, the Eagle that Went to War

Civil War battlefields were a long way from Wisconsin, but many Badger State soldiers fought valiantly for the Union cause. The Eighth Wisconsin Regiment was inspired by an extraordinary mascot, a bald eagle captured north of Jim Falls in 1861. Named Old Abe, the great bird went with them in thirty-nine battles, held above the troops on a special red, white, and blue perch. The screeching, flapping eagle was inspiring for the Wisconsin troops and daunting for the enemy. Soon the Eighth was known as the "Eagle Regiment."

Another unique aspect of the Eighth Wisconsin's history centers around a twenty-six-year-old red-haired major named John Jefferson who rose to command the regiment. Active in capital politics in Madison, Jefferson had been a member of the elite Governor's Guard militia. He was wounded at Corinth and Vicksburg. After the war he returned to Tennessee and became a wealthy Memphis cotton merchant. DNA tests have now shown that he was the grandson of Thomas Jefferson and his slave mistress, Sally Hemings.

Amazingly, Old Abe survived the war and lived until 1881. He had a special apartment in the State Capitol in Madison, where visiting children would patiently wait for him to shed a souvenir feather. He became close to the state armorer and would perch gently on his outstretched arm and affectionately rub his head against the armorer's cheek. Old Abe was often reunited with his Civil War comrades at parades and rallies.

The waters of the Chippewa River are ideal places for eagles to swoop down on unsuspecting fish. If you're lucky you'll spot some members of Old Abe's gene pool soaring above the valley. If not, you'll have to be satisfied with a photo op in front of the giant statue of Old Abe in Jim Falls.

17 OMAHA TRAIL

You'll pass through a block-and-a-half-long railroad tunnel and exquisite bluff country scenery along the Omaha Trail. Near Mill Bluff State Park, it connects to a 100-mile rail trail system.

Activities:

Location: Elroy to Camp Douglas

Length: 13.9 miles

Surface: Seal-coated gravel with short sections of crushed gravel at each end

Wheelchair access: Yes

Precautions: Crossings at some gravel roads are unpaved. An ice mound builds up in the middle of the tunnel and typically lasts into early summer. Short on-street sections connect the northern and southern trailheads. Bikers should watch for vertical barriers at trail intersections, which are easily passed but no fun if run into. A $1.00 daily or $5.00 annual Juneau County trail pass fee is required for adult bicyclists. (This is different from the Wisconsin State Trail Pass needed for the connecting Elroy-Sparta and "400" State Trails.) Passes can be purchased at Elroy Commons, the Hustle Stop convenience store in Hustler, the Target Bluff German Haus Restaurant in Camp Douglas, and at some other area businesses. In winter you must have a Wisconsin snowmobile registration or nonresident trail use sticker.

Food and facilities: There are restaurants in Elroy, including one next to the Elroy Commons trailhead. There is a convenience store on Main Street in Hustler. There is a restaurant at the Camp Douglas trailhead, and taverns in all trail towns. Water and flush toilets are at the Elroy Commons trailhead and at the trailside park in Hustler. Elroy Commons also has shower. Water and clean pit toilets are at the north end of the tunnel. There is a swimming pool on the south side of Elroy at Schultz Park and a swimming beach at Mill Bluff State Park, 3 miles west of Camp Douglas. Playgrounds are at Elroy Commons and in Hustler.

Seasons: Open year-round

124 Best Rail Trails Wisconsin

Access and parking: At the northern end in Camp Douglas, the trail starts 0.2 mile east of Interstate 90/94 at the parking lot next to the Target Bluff German Haus Restaurant on U.S. Highway 12/ Wisconsin Highway16. At the southern end in Elroy, the recommended trailhead is at the Elroy Commons between Main Street (Wisconsin Highway 82/80) and Railroad Street just north of Franklin Street (County Road O). Shuttle service is offered by Speed's Bicycle Sales ad Service in Sparta.

Rentals: Elroy Commons, (608) 462–2410. Speed's Bicycle Sales and Service, Sparta, (608) 269–2315. Target Bluff German Haus, (608) 427–6542.

Contact: Elroy Commons Bike Trails and Tourist Information, (608) 462–2410, www.elroywi.com. Juneau County Land, Forestry and Parks Department, (608) 847–9389.

This is a trail with a tunnel of the tamer type. Any railroad tunnel is impressive, and the one on the Omaha Trail is no exception. But compared to the tunnels on the connecting Elroy-Sparta State Trail, the Omaha Trail's tunnel is tiny. It is only about half the length of the two short Elroy-Sparta tunnels, and less than a fourth as long as the monstrous Tunnel #3. For bikers, the upside of the Omaha Trail tunnel's size is that you can ride through it—if you are skilled and brave.

There is more to the Omaha Trail than the tunnel. Laid out for the Omaha Line, the rail grade passes superb scenery. It includes rock formations that won't be seen anywhere else for a thousand miles. There are interesting museums at Camp Douglas and Elroy, and if you haven't been in Hustler at least once in your life, well, you haven't been anywhere.

The Omaha Trail is one of a collection of rail trails that junction in Elroy. These include the Elroy-Sparta State Trail to the west and the "400" State Trail to the south. Two things differentiate the Omaha Trail from the others. The Omaha is not a state trail; it is owned and maintained by Juneau County and has its own trail-pass fees. And it has a more all-weather surface than the crushed limestone on the state trails. The Omaha Trail is surfaced with seal-coated gravel, which is hard like asphalt, but not smooth enough

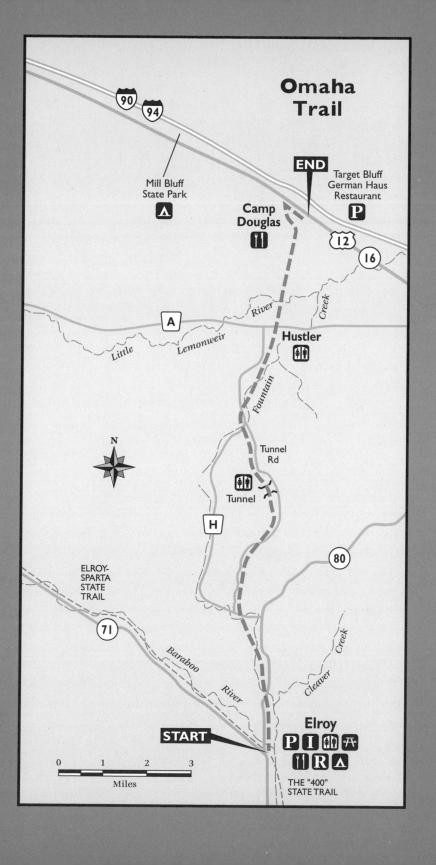

Omaha Trail

90 94

Mill Bluff
State Park

END

Target Bluff
German Haus
Restaurant

P

Camp
Douglas

12

16

River

Creek

A

Little *Lemonweir*

Hustler

Fountain

N

Tunnel
Rd

Tunnel

H

80

ELROY-
SPARTA
STATE
TRAIL

71

Baraboo

River

Cleaver Creek

Elroy

P I

R

START

0   1   2   3
Miles

THE "400"
STATE TRAIL

for in-line skating. It does make it the trail of choice if it has rained recently because the seal coat dries off much faster than the crushed stone.

Restored railroad buildings at Elroy Commons serve as a trailhead for all three trails that junction in town. A cafe across Railroad Street from the commons buildings keeps visitors from having to walk too far for refreshments. If you return to Elroy on a weekend afternoon, you may want to check out the Museum on Main. Located in an impressive Gothic brick building on Main Street, the museum has exhibits on farm and town life from yesteryear, including a display showing early-twentieth-century Elroy in miniature when the railroads were thriving.

Traveling north from Elroy Commons, you'll need to follow the "400" State Trail and streets a short distance to get to the Omaha Trail, following brown and white direction signs. Follow the north extension of the "400" State Trail from the Elroy Commons buildings for 0.2 mile until it T intersects with Cedar Street and turn left (west). Go a quarter block to Second Main Street and turn right (north). At 0.4 mile, at the intersection with Ninth Street, continue straight onto the Omaha Trail and cross the covered bridge.

At 1.1 miles the trail crosses WI 80/82. You are in Sherman Valley, which is narrow everywhere but is widest here. Through gaps in the trailside brush you may catch sight of a herd of grazing horses.

At 3.1 miles you cross County Road H. Now the trail will closely parallel the aptly named Tunnel Road until you cross H again north of the tunnel. You'll really get a feel for the advantage of the railroad grade as you see this gravel road rising and dropping with the contours of the land. At 3.6 miles the trail does a funny double crossing of a sharp bend in the road.

The valley becomes narrower and narrower as you gradually climb the 120 feet to the tunnel. The passage becomes almost viselike as you near the entrance. If you're biking and brave enough to try riding through it, you should have a fat-tired bike. The tunnel floor is firm sand, but thin tires will bog down in it. Another potential obstacle is ice, at least in spring and early summer. Water dripping from the roof freezes in the middle of the tunnel, forming an uneven hump. It is a good idea to walk over it. This is surprisingly easy because the sand on your shoes gives good traction.

At 7.0 miles, outside the north tunnel entrance, there is a picnic area with a water pump. Kids love to get the pump going, which can be a work-

Kids love to work the water pump near the Omaha Trail tunnel.

out for anybody. A half mile later you'll see Tunnel Road again. It had disappeared up over the hill before the south entrance. At 8.5 miles, as the valley begins to widen, Tunnel Road drops away to junction with County Road H. At this point the railroad grade passes over the county road on a 40-foot-high bridge. Then, just a third of a mile later, it makes a grade-level crossing of the same road.

The trail is following Fountain Creek on its way to the little village of Hustler, "The One and Only in the World," a good place to mail a postcard from. Nearing the village, the trail enters the broad valley of the Lemonweir River. Hustler may be good for a joke, but it really has a nice little park with a modern playground alongside the trail.

North of Hustler the trail continues in the wide valley, although trees and brush along the trail keep it intimate. Straight ahead you'll see a bluff with a fire lookout tower on top. The bluff is actually on the north side of I–90/94 at Camp Douglas. It is one of the most stunning sights on the interstate, along with nearby Castle Rock and Target Bluff. The crags and towers of these huge buff-colored sandstone rocks began as islands in Glacial

Lake Wisconsin, a body of dammed-up meltwater the size of Green Bay. Since then, wind and weather have given the many bluffs and outcroppings in the area a distinctly western look. Time has worked ancient stone into wonderful shapes. Dwarf prickly pear cactus grows on the thin sandy soil. Technically, the 80- to 200-foot-high bluffs in this area are mesas, a feature usually found in the western United States. You wouldn't see any again until you hit the Dakotas.

The trail bends to the northwest at 12.1 miles, just before entering Camp Douglas. In town it ends abruptly just before Main Street (County Road H) at 13.5 miles. Blue and white bike trail signs guide you east on Washburn Street, then to the southeast end of Douglas Street at 13.7 miles, where you continue straight (southeast) onto a crushed limestone trail. The trail swings around to the northeast in the shadow of Target Bluff, once used by railroad engineers to sight the line as they ran the rails up from New Lisbon. At 13.9 miles you arrive at the parking lot on the south side of the Target Bluff German Haus Restaurant.

Camp Douglas has several points of interest. The Wisconsin National Guard Museum is located just north of town at the Fort Williams National Guard Base. Three miles west of town on US 12/WI 16 is Mill Bluff State Park, where you can hike to the top of a mesa overlooking the endless traffic flow on I–90/94 and the towering rectangular pinnacle of Bee Bluff to the north. The rock formations at the park make it well worth a visit, but it's not the greatest place to camp. The background noise of I–90/94 is punctuated by frequent Soo Line freight trains that run all night and sound their air horns at the County Road W crossing.

18 OSAUGIE TRAIL

The Osaugie Trail features great views of the Twin Ports harbor, interesting museums and historic sites, and city services.

Activities:

Note: ATVs run parallel to the trail on a gravel track along the north side of the trail east of the Burlington Ore Dock.

Location: Superior

Length: 5.2 miles

Surface: Asphalt

Wheelchair access: Yes

Precautions: Some sections of the trail are in need of maintenance and showing potholes. There are many crossings at city streets, as well as two gravel crossings at active railroad tracks and one at an abandoned railroad grade. There are several steep sections. The bridge at Bluff Creek is surfaced with planks laid parallel to the trail. Narrow gaps between planks may cause problems for bicycles with thin tires. The trail may be heavily used for many types of recreation on summer weekends. In winter you must have a Wisconsin snowmobile registration or nonresident trail use sticker.

Food and facilities: Services too numerous to mention are close at hand in Superior. Along the trail itself you'll find restrooms, water, and a playground at Harbor View Park at the Osaugie Trail trailhead. At 23rd Avenue there is a McDonald's 1 block south at the corner of 23rd and U.S. Highway 2. The unique Choo Choo Pub & Grill, a tavern/restaurant in a 1930s railroad car, is on 50th Street across US 2. There are porta-type toilets and a modern playground at Bear Creek Park at the Moccasin Mike Road trail terminus.

Seasons: Open year-round

Access and parking: From Interstate 535 at the south end of the Blatnik Bridge, take the U.S. Highway 53 exit south. US 53 becomes Harbor View Parkway. Harbor View Park is on the north side of US 53 at the intersection of Belknap Street (US 2).

Rentals: Deco Bay Fun 4 Rent, (715) 392–1495

Contact: Superior and Douglas County Convention and Visitors Bureau, (800) 942–5313 or (715) 392–2773

|||||||||||||||||||||||||||||||||||||||||||||||||||||||||||||||||||||||||||||||||||||||||

Superior's new Osaugie Trail gives visitors a great view of the Twin Ports harbor, the busiest and biggest on the Great Lakes. Superior and its sister city, Duluth, Minnesota, are the gateway to the nation and the world for the bounty of the Midwest. Grain goes to countries all over the world. Iron ore is destined for America's steel mills. All ships must pass over the treacherous waters of Lake Superior, the greatest of the Great Lakes. It is the world's largest body of fresh water, the fabled Gitche Gumee of Ojibwe legend.

Superior has lots to offer the visitor in the way of restaurants, shopping, and attractions. The Old Firehouse Museum and Fairlawn Museum are close to the trail. Two Wisconsin state parks, Pattison and Amnicon Falls, are outside the city. Pattison is the site of the highest waterfall in the state.

The western trailhead is at Harbor View Park, which has a nice modern playground. Here you will also find the Richard I. Bong WWII Heritage Center. Bong was a local boy who became America's top fighter ace in World War II. The actual Lockheed Lightning P38 he flew is housed in the museum. The trail is easily identified by aqua-painted steel Osaugie Trail arches.

Traveling east from Harbor View Park, you head downhill 0.1 mile to a junction with a railroad-bed portion of the trail. To the west the trail dead-ends after 0.3 mile, where it awaits future development. Following the trail east, you'll pass Barker's Island. There you'll see the cigar-shaped SS *Meteor*, the last of the whaleback freighters. The ship, launched in 1896, was one of many built in Superior. Its submarine-like hull was designed to withstand the pounding of the lake. It is a floating museum that can be toured daily from mid-May to September.

At 0.7 mile is Marina Drive, which leads to the SS *Meteor*. Here the trail crosses the road and leaves the rail bed. It swings south then east

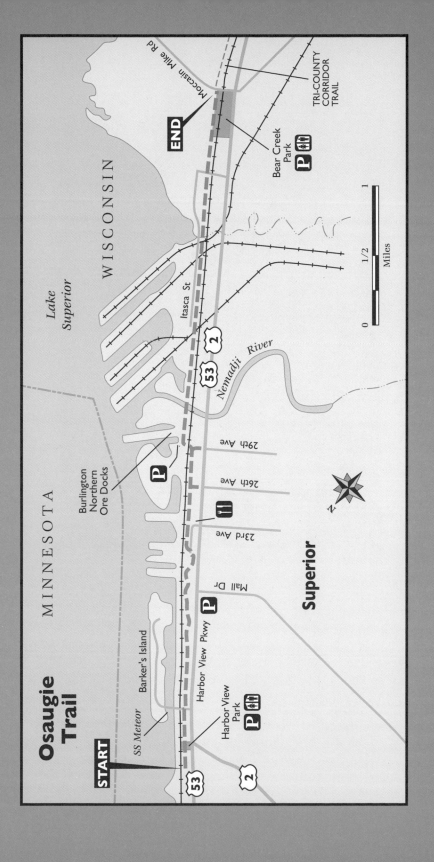

Osaugie Trail

START

MINNESOTA

SS Meteor

Barker's Island

Burlington
Northern
Ore Docks

Harbor View Pkwy

Mall Dr

23rd Ave

26th Ave

29th Ave

Superior

Harbor View
Park

P

P

P

Lake
Superior

WISCONSIN

Nemadji River

Itasca St

53

2

Moccasin Mike Rd

END

Bear Creek
Park

P

TRI-COUNTY
CORRIDOR
TRAIL

53

2

N

0   1/2   1
Miles

An in-line skater rolls past the SS Meteor *along Barker's Island.*

as it climbs up to the level of US 2/53. The trail then follows the gently rolling natural terrain. At 1.1 miles you reach a small park with a gazebo shelter and picnic tables at a spot that was the site of the Superior Stockade during the Civil War. At 1.3 miles the trail makes a steep descent as it swings to the north. At 1.6 miles the trail crosses 22nd Avenue East and makes an immediate turn northeast, crossing gravel and active railroad tracks. Immediately after the crossing, the trail turns to the southeast and resumes traveling on a railroad grade.

The trail passes through a low-lying area, and at 1.9 miles it crosses a marsh on a boardwalk. Just southeast of the boardwalk, at 2.0 miles, there is a gravel crossing of an abandoned railroad grade. At 2.1 miles a spur trail splits off the southwest to 26th Avenue East; 0.3 mile later another spur trail goes southwest to 29th Avenue East. At 2.5 miles the trail swings to the northeast to another gravel crossing of an active railroad line. Immediately after the crossing, the trail turns southeast once again, and at 2.6 miles it exits into a parking area at the historic Burlington Northern Ore Docks.

At the southeast end of the parking lot at 2.7 miles, the Osaugie Trail passes under the massive Burlington Northern Ore Docks. Iron ore from Minnesota's Mesabi Range has been loaded here for more than one hundred years. Half of all the ore used for World War II production came from the Mesabi. The dock was where the huge lake freighter the *Edmund Fitzgerald* took on its load of taconite ore before it met its fate in the terrible Lake Superior storm of November 10, 1975. The *Edmund Fitz* went down with all twenty-nine crewmen. No one in the Twin Ports forgets the anniversary of the sinking.

After passing under the ore dock, the trail again travels on a railroad grade. At 3.0 miles you'll cross the twisting Nemadji River. The trail passes under an active ore dock at 3.4 miles, then runs parallel to Itasca Street until 4.1 miles, where it crosses Bluff Creek.

At 5.3 miles the Osaugie Trail junctions with Moccasin Mike Road at Bear Creek Park, where you'll find a nice, modern little playground. This is the end of the Osaugie and the beginning of the Tri-County Corridor Trail, a gravel and natural-surface multiuse rail trail that runs east to the city of Ashland, Wisconsin. The Tri-County has not been very popular with non-motorized users because it is an ATV trail in spring, summer, and fall. Two other interesting area rail trails to check out are the Lakewalk Trail and the Willard Munger Trail on the Minnesota side of the harbor.

19 OZAUKEE INTERURBAN TRAIL

Pass through farmland and small-town Wisconsin as you follow the path of the former electric railway across the county and cross the Cedar Creek bridge in historic Cedarburg.

Activities:

Location: Ozaukee-Milwaukee County line to Ozaukee-Sheboygan County line

Length: 29.9 miles with some on-road segments

Surface: Crushed stone; asphalt segments in Port Washington and Cedarburg

Wheelchair access: Yes

Precautions: There are crossings at numerous streets and some on-road portions.

Food and facilities: Belgium, Port Washington, Grafton, Cedarburg, Thiensville, and Mequon all have restaurants, cafes, and taverns close to the trail. Village Park in Belgium, Lions Comfort Station and Lake Park in Port Washington, Veterans Memorial Park in Grafton, Community Center Gym in Cedarburg, and the Logemann Community Center in Mequon all have restrooms and water. There are public pools in Mequon and Grafton.

Seasons: Open year-round

Access and parking: From Interstate 43, take the Wisconsin Highway 57 exit and go west 3.3 miles on Wisconsin Highway 57/167 to the Logemann Community Center where there is a parking lot.

Rentals: Extreme Ski and Bike, Thiensville, (262) 242–1442, www.extreme skiandbike.com. Grafton Ski and Cyclery, (262) 377–5220. Port Ski and Cyclery, (262) 268–9808.

Contact: Mequon-Thiensville Chamber of Commerce, (262) 512–9358. Cedarburg Visitor Center, (800) 237–2874. Grafton Chamber of Commerce, (262) 377–1650. Port Washington Tourism, (800) 719–4881. Belgium Chamber of Commerce, (262) 285–7887, www.interurbantrail.us.

The imposing Cedarburg Mill overlooks the Ozaukee Interurban Trail.

With our current environmental concerns, much is being said about the use of electric-powered transportation. Oddly enough, Milwaukee had already gone that direction over one hundred years ago, and it was the rise of the automobile, in fact, that brought about the end of interurban electric train lines out of the Cream City.

The Milwaukee system operated from 1905 to 1951, but the line through Ozaukee County, called the Northern Route, ran out of juice by 1948. The train stopped in each of the communities you will pass through on this trail. Hourly trains took passengers north all the way to Sheboygan. The line gained notoriety for bringing hopeful African-American blues musicians to the Paramount recording studios in Port Washington and later in Grafton. Today's multiuse trail follows this historic railway's former path.

The trail begins at the Milwaukee and Ozaukee county line on the aptly named County Line Road 0.4 mile west of WI 57. The Brown Deer Recreation Trail continues south from here. Heading north at 0.5 mile, you

go over a small creek and then at 1.0 mile cross Donges Bay Road. Another mile brings you to Mequon Road, where you can use the parking lot at the Logemann Community Center to your right (north) on Mequon Road (also WI 167). This is perhaps a better starting point than the actual trailhead, where there is no official parking area.

Continuing north, cross Division Street at 2.2 miles and Bunt Rock at 2.5 miles as you pass behind local businesses and some apartment complexes. Pass over a small creek on a bridge at 2.8 miles. Mequon Community Park is to your right and offers a playground, a public pool, restrooms, and water just on the other side of the baseball diamond. Just past the park in the strip mall to your right is Extreme Ski and Bike, which rents bicycles. At Freistadt Road, the next crossing, there are places to your right offering refreshments, specifically a Walgreens and a gas station one intersection over.

Soon after leaving Mequon/Thiensville, you'll pass over a small bridge at 3.4 miles, and 0.5 mile later you'll cross Highland Road. Cross Pigeon Creek on a bridge at 4.0 miles. The trail now runs alongside Cedarburg Road until it crosses the railroad tracks to your left. Chain-link fences are staggered here to ensure that bikers don't simply rush across what is an active rail route. You'll pass a power booster station on your left at 4.7 miles, and then the trail curves left steeply. Be careful of bicyclists flying downhill from the other direction and around this corner.

After the next road crossing at Bonniwell Road, the trail is bordered by thick brush and trees, which make it seem much more rural than it is. When you see the soccer fields on your left, you are almost to Cedarburg; you will cross Pioneer Road at 6.1 miles. You'll cross Alyce Street and then the much busier Lincoln Boulevard as the path winds through residences into town. Just after the big Cedarburg water tower, the trail crosses Western Road at 7.0 miles.

The path comes out on Center Street and continues on local streets. Go right on Center Street just 200 feet. At 7.2 miles you'll come to Hanover Avenue; go left, passing the library and post office. From Hanover Avenue just past Turner Street at 7.4 miles, the trail heads right and crosses the block to Washington Avenue. To your right just next to the trail, serving some great Italian pie by the slice, is Sal's Pizzeria, with sidewalk seating. Washington Avenue hosts a lot of shops and restaurants, and just a half block south is the impressive downtown center of Cedarburg, which is worth exploring. You can visit the 1855 Cedarburg Mill on Portland Road and Columbia Road. Go around back to the Silver Creek Brewpub to see the flowing creek up close and have snacks after 5:00 p.m.

Back on the trail at 7.5 miles, you will cross a large steel-truss bridge over Cedar Creek. Look to your right to find the old Cedarburg Mill. A sign at the foot of the bridge tells the story of the electric railway that once used to cross here. At the east end of the bridge, the path runs through the fire station parking lot, crosses Mequon Avenue, and a block later, Jefferson Avenue.

At 7.8 miles you'll pass a cemetery on your left before crossing Bridge Street and Hawthorne at an angle. At 8.0 miles you'll be at Cedar Ridge Drive, and another 0.3 mile later you'll find a trail map as you cross Keup Road. Trail traffic is moderate between Grafton and Cedarburg and includes commuters as well as recreational users.

From First Avenue in Grafton begins the so-called River Loop, though it really doesn't offer much in the way of river views. For the alternate "through route," which involves fewer turns and street connections, go left at First Avenue and take it north 0.9 mile to North Street. Go right 0.6 mile to rejoin the asphalt trail on your left just past the railroad crossing. Watch for the route signs.

The River Loop, however, stays off road for another 0.4 mile after which you will take a left onto Seventh Avenue. From here it's 0.3 mile to Beech Street, where you take a right at 0.2 mile to 11th Avenue. Go north on this another 0.4 mile and turn left onto North Street. The trail resumes off road on your right. Continue another 0.5 mile to cross Hickory Street.

Now to your right is Meadowbrook Park and Family Aquatic Center with a playground, parking, restrooms, water, and a public pool. At the end of the park, you will also find a bike rack and map board trailside just as you hit 11.1 miles and the County Road O crossing. The trail resumes on the other side. At 11.2 miles cross the bridge over the Milwaukee River. The trail rises slightly into forest 0.3 mile later.

You'll come to the intersection of Terminal Road and East River Road at 12.1 miles. Watch the signage carefully because plans are in the works to reroute the trail, taking it off road past a golf course and through some wetlands and hardwood forest as it takes a pedestrian bridge over I–43.

This will convert approximately 2 miles of on-road trail to an off-road segment of 1.3 miles.

For now go right on Terminal Road 0.5 mile over the hill to County Road W. Go left another 0.5 mile to Ulao Parkway and take it right, crossing I–43 at 13.2 miles. Watch for Ridgewood Road 0.4 mile on your left. Go left on Ridgewood Road through a residential neighborhood for 0.9 mile and you will find the path again on your right. This is where the future I–43 overpass bridge trail should rejoin the trail.

As you approach Port Washington, cross Sauk Road at 14.9 miles and enjoy the cool shade as the trail passes through thick woods. At 15.1 miles the trail opens to the sky again. Cross County Road LL and Sunset Drive, both at an angle. At 16.2 miles the trail descends to the intersection of Portview Road and Spring Drive. You will cross at the crosswalks over Spring Drive and pick up the trail on the other side heading (left) northeast. It's 0.3 mile to Oakland Avenue where the trail goes on the street. Go right on Oakland Avenue for 0.3 mile until you reach Keeney Street. Take a left and pass a cemetery on your left. Go left on the next street on your left, Chestnut Street, and just a half block later, go right on a short wide road immmediately before Park Street. It's just a couple of hundred feet and then right again at the next corner that the asphalt trail resumes, heading slightly downhill to cross Webster Street and bring you to a long,m narrow parking lot.

This is an official trail lot, and there are restrooms and water at the Lions Comfort Station. Picnic tables offer a place to take a break as well, and there is a map board. You'll come out of the parking lot at 17.6 miles on Wisconsin Avenue and follow it left across a bridge over Sauk Creek. Turn right on Grand Avenue at the traffic lights and follow it to where it ends in a corner with Franklin Street. Go left on Franklin for 3 blocks. There are many shops, restaurants, and taverns through here. Turn right on Pier Street, go 1 block, and head left at Harborview Lane, also following it for only 1 block. Go right on Jackson Street, and a half block later you will see the trail and trail board on your left shortly before you arrive at the marina. Veterans Memorial Park and Lake Park are just past the trail going left on Lake Street. From here the trail gets some partial shade and also more users. A creek flows alongside the trail to the right, and you can hear the water burbling as you pass.

At 18.6 miles you'll pass a wide mowed area to your left just as you approach Hales Trail. Cross this street and go straight, following a short section of Kaiser Drive to the end, where the asphalt trail picks up again. From here you will cross several residential streets and pass the back of a school on your left as you approach the final in-town crossing.

When you come to Seven Hills Road (County Road LL), there is a crosswalk. Go to the other side and head right on the asphalt path. The Ozaukee County Park and Ride is to the left of this crossing, and there is a Sentry Foods visible from here as well.

The sidewalk path ends, and the next 0.2 mile is on Seven Hills Road. Turn left onto Highland Lane to pass under I–43. This is a short connecting road to the other side of the highway, and you'll immediately turn left on Highland Road and follow it as it curves right toward the west. At 20.7 miles you cross over a bridge, and you'll see the trail descends just past it on the left. It will circle back around and under the bridge and start heading north again on an off-road crushed-limestone path through farmland.

When you arrive at Belgium, you'll find a couple of places to eat along Main Street. There are parking, toilets, and water at Village Park. To arrive there, go east on Main Street to Beech Street and the park is on your left.

The trail continues across Main Street and slightly to the right of the trail you are leaving. It curves to the left to resume on the old rail path. The last 3.5-mile segment from Belgium to the county line passes through more unshaded farmland and some small patches of wetlands. This trail ends at the county line on County Road K just alongside tracks at a stop sign. Plans, however, are to continue developing the trail all the way to Sheboygan. There is no official parking here.

20 RED CEDAR STATE TRAIL

Bald eagle sightings are common throughout the year. Great river scenery and an 860-foot long trestle are highlights of the trail, along with the historic city of Menomonie, two quaint small river villages, and a ghost town

Activities:

Note: Snowshoeing is allowed south of Downsville only

Location: Menomonie to the Chippewa River State Trail

Length: 14.2 miles

Surface: Crushed limestone with wood-planked bridges; groomed and tracked for cross-country skiing from Menomonie to Downsville

Wheelchair access: No

Precautions: There are no services between Downsville and the southern end of the trail. Wisconsin State Trails have a carry-in/carry-out policy. Make provisions for carrying out any refuse. No trash receptacles are provided on-trail. The Wisconsin State Trail Pass is required for bicyclists age sixteen and older ($4.00 daily or $20.00 annually). The trail pass also covers usage such as cross-country skiing, horseback riding, and bicycling on state mountain bike trails and other rail trails. Passes can be purchased at the Depot Visitor Information Center in Menomonie and at self-pay stations at trail access parking lots.

Food and facilities: You will find all services in Menomonie. There are flush toilets and water at the trailhead Depot Visitor Information Center in Menomonie. The Depot Visitor Information Center is open May through October, but only on weekends in May, September, and October. There is a tavern in Irvington, and there are taverns, a country store, a restaurant, and seasonal trailside flush toilets in Downsville.

Seasons: Open year-round

Access and parking: From Interstate 94, take Wisconsin Highway 25 south into Menomonie and turn right (west) on Wisconsin Highway 29 (11th Avenue). The trailhead depot parking lot is 0.4 mile on the left.

Rentals: Roscoe's Red Cedar Outfitters, Menomonie, (715) 231–8735. Simple Sports, Menomonie, (715) 233–3493.

Contact: Chippewa Valley Convention and Visitors Bureau, (888) 523–3866, www.chippewavalley.net. Red Cedar State Trail, (715) 232–1242.

|||||||||||||||||||||||||||||||||||||||||||||||||||||||||||||||||||||||||||||||||||

The city of Menomonie is an ideal trailhead location for the Red Cedar State Trail. In addition to many dining and lodging options, it has a rich history, much of it tied to Knapp, Stout & Company, once the largest lumber business in the world. Mill money built many beautiful homes and endowed a college, now UW Stout. The Mabel Tainter Theater is part of that legacy. Located right downtown, the ornate castlelike building features live performances periodically throughout the winter. Built in 1891 for the then astounding sum of $105,000, it is open Monday through Saturday for self-guided tours.

Nearby, Dunn County's Russell J. Rassbach Heritage Museum, open Wednesday through Sunday afternoon, showcases local history. Included are displays of Victorian period rooms, Civil War artifacts, an early plastic thermoform machine, a 1931 Nash sedan, and a 1900 Submerged Electric Motor Company outboard motor.

Whether you ski, snowshoe, bike, or hike, you are in for adventure and beautiful scenery on the Red Cedar State Trail. The northern half from Menomonie to Downsville is specially tracked and groomed for both classic and skate-skiing techniques. South of Downsville you may snowshoe or ski, but there is no special trail grooming.

Heading south from the Depot Visitor Information Center trailhead, you plunge into a cool, deep hardwood forest. At 0.3 mile you cross a wood-planked iron bridge over tree-sheltered Gilbert Creek. Shortly after, the trail emerges from the woods and runs close to the surging Red Cedar River. Keep an eye out for bald eagles anytime you are near the river. They love to soar above it. If you're lucky, you'll spot one swooping down to catch a fish.

At 1.3 miles the trail is sandwiched between the river and a tall sandstone bluff. If you visit in winter or early spring, you will find ice falls in this

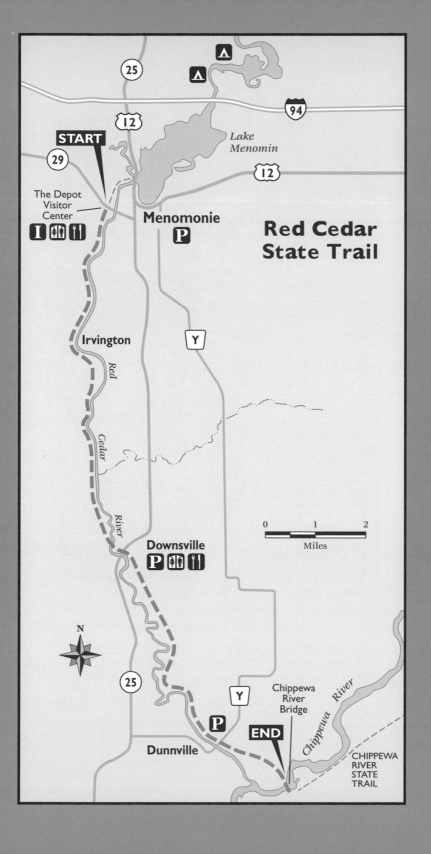

Red Cedar State Trail

25

⛺
⛺

94

12

Lake Menomin

12

29

START

The Depot Visitor Center

ℹ️ 🚻 🍴

Menomonie

P

Irvington

Red

Y

Cedar

River

0   1   2
Miles

Downsville

P 🚻 🍴

N

25

Y

Chippewa River Bridge

Chippewa River

P

END

Dunnville

CHIPPEWA RIVER STATE TRAIL

The Red Cedar River runs close to the trail.

sheltered spot. Water dripping from the top freezes into fantastic forms, growing larger with each thaw and freeze.

You'll reach Irvington at 3.0 miles. The only business in the tiny community is the Trailside Tavern. Check out the social scene if the euchre players are dealing the cards when you visit. The food is basic bar fare, but the old mechanical bowling game is worth a try.

Traveling south, the trail leaves the river edge and crosses open fields. At about 4.0 miles, look for bald eagle nests high in the treetops to the west. At 4.5 miles the trail returns to the river and remains alongside it until 6.4 miles. The river begins to bend in this section. This meandering character will be more typical of the Red Cedar for the rest of its length. A river bend at 7.2 miles is where the trail crosses to the east side on a fine old stressed-iron bridge.

Compared to Irvington, Downsville, at the 7.5-mile point, seems huge. It has two taverns, a country grocery, and a post office. Cards postmarked Downsville are collector's items if you are "hip" to the lingo of the '50s Beat. T.J.'s Tavern is known for its Friday night fish fries, and the Country Zone has great pizza, but the premier place to eat is the Creamery. Located on the east end of town on County Road C, it has elegant lodging and a wonderful lunch and dinner menu. Considering this town's diminutive size, it has an impressive variety of excellent food.

Downsville was once a boomtown as a stop for lumber rafts floating from Menomonie's sawmills down to the Chippewa and Mississippi Rivers. It still looks much as it must have a century ago. The Empire in the Pines Museum is open in the summer Friday through Sunday from noon to 5:00 p.m. There you can see how the lumberjacks lived. It wasn't an easy life.

South of Downsville the rail bed runs to the east of the river until it nearly touches the apex of a sharp bend at 8.0 miles. You are now entering a section where ice falls are common. Just a bit farther, at 8.7 miles, the trail begins running next to the river again, following a broad bend for 0.7 mile.

The next town on the trail isn't there anymore. Dunnville, at the County Road Y crossing at 12.3 miles, is a ghost town. It once thrived on the river traffic and was even the county seat. You may be able to spot a remnant of the old stagecoach road climbing the east side of the valley, but that is the only evidence of Dunnville that remains.

Now the trail has left the valley of the Red Cedar and crosses the broad floodplain of the Chippewa River. A mile and a half to two miles wide in most places, the valley leaves plenty of room for the river to meander at will. Protected as the Dunnville State Wildlife Area, the bottoms are a great place to spot red-tailed hawks.

Ahead lies one of the great rail trail river crossings in the state. At 14.0 miles you'll cross the Chippewa River on a massive 860-foot-long

The iron bridge at Downsville in a good place to stop for a view of the Red Cedar River.

stressed-iron railroad trestle. Great views up and down the river valley are guaranteed. At the south end, at 14.2 miles, the Red Cedar State Trail joins the Chippewa River State Trail, which gives direct access to the city of Eau Claire 21 miles to the east.

Both the Red Cedar and Chippewa River State Trails are part of the Great Wisconsin Binding and Nature Trail Program.

21 SOUTHWEST PATH

Activities:

Location: Madison

Length: 5.7 miles

Surface: Asphalt

Wheelchair access: Yes

Precautions: There are crossings at numerous streets throughout the trail, several of which can be quite busy.

Food and facilities: The first half of this trail passes through downtown, where a variety of restaurants and bars sit just off the trail a few blocks in either direction. However, past the football stadium there are almost no on-trail facilities.

Seasons: Open year-round

Access and parking: Follow U.S. Highway 151 south from East Washington as it becomes John Nolen Drive. At the intersection of North Shore Drive, go right. On your left is a parking lot just before the Brittingham Park boathouse. There is no parking lot at the end of the trail, but there are many access points along the path where street parking is permitted.

Rentals: Williamson Bikes and Fitness, (608) 255–5292, www.willybikes .com. Machinery Row Bicycles, (608) 442–5974, www.machineryrow bicycles.com. Yellow Jersey, (608) 257–4737, www.yellowjersey.org.

Contact: Greater Madison Convention and Visitors Bureau, (608) 255–2537 or (800) 373–6376, www.visitmadison.com. City of Madison Pedestrian-Bicycle Coordinator, (608) 266–6225, www.cityofmadison.com.

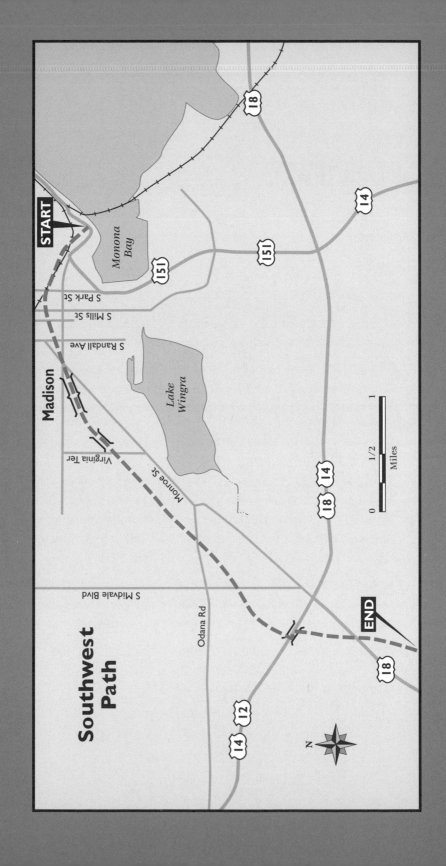

Also known as the Southwest Commuter Path, this nicely paved and heavily traveled trail clearly serves more than just recreational purposes. It follows right along the downtown corridor and just south of the University of Wisconsin. It is also a bit of a cutoff trail for bicyclists trying to reach the Military Ridge State Trail from the Capital City Trail; the Southwest Path takes 6.2 miles off the Capital City Trail's connection from Lake Monona to the access trail to the Military Ridge Trail. Bikers can have a snicker at rush-hour traffic, which typically cannot get from downtown to the near west side as quickly or efficiently. On Badger game days this is a straight shot to Camp Randall Stadium from either end of the trail. And if you are merely out for a short pleasure ride, the railroad corridor heading southwest from the stadium is rich with shade trees and flower gardens.

The parking lot at Brittingham Park has picnic tables and portable toilets. The park is very popular for fishing along the shoreline of Monona Bay. The Capital City Trail is close by on the lake side of John Nolen Drive just 0.2 mile northeast along North Shore Drive. For the Southwest Path, start from the parking lot and go left past the boathouse with Monona Bay to your left. You will reach a double-wide pedestrian crosswalk going to the right across North Shore Drive. This is the trailhead. Cross and begin down the asphalt path into the city.

The trail follows along the right side of the railroad tracks for the first 2 blocks, then at Doty Street crosses to the other side. At 0.3 mile you come to West Washington Avenue, where you will cross a sometimes very busy four-lane road. There are traffic lights 300 feet to the left if you find it too busy to cross.

The Capitol is visible up Washington Avenue to your right. On the other side of the street on the right is Williamson Bikes and Fitness in the old train depot. Also near the depot is a row of Milwaukee Road passenger cars with shops inside.

The path continues behind local businesses and apartments to the left. At about 0.5 mile on your right, you'll see the Kohl Center, where the University of Wisconsin men's and women's basketball and hockey teams play. It is also a popular venue for big-name concerts. There are exits off the trail to Maya Street to your left, and passageways go under the bike path and railroad tracks to the Kohl Center grounds.

At 0.7 mile a bridge with fences on either side will take you over Park

Street. At 0.9 mile the path crosses Mills Street, and you can see a large coal-burning power plant to your right. The active tracks to your right are for freight trains hauling coal.

At the end of this block, you will cross Spring Street at an angle, just barely running over the opposite corner of the street before crossing Charter Street. A block later at 1.0 mile, you'll cross Orchard Street. At 1.1 miles the trail meets Randall Avenue. To your right is a popular sports hang-out, the Stadium Bar, which serves good bar food. A half block to your left at the next traffic light is a convenience store. Go straight across Randall with the trail; Camp Randall Stadium is to your right.

The 80,000-seat stadium is, of course, home to the Wisconsin Badgers. During the Civil War this was the site of a Union Army base. Former Wisconsin governor Alexander Randall rallied troops for the war, and so the camp took his name. On football game days, this area is a sea of red as fans adorned in school colors fill the stadium and the surrounding bars.

At 1.3 miles you approach your most complicated crossing, the busiest intersection on the trail. Cross Monroe to your right, stopping at the small concrete island before the right-turn lane, and then take a left across Regent. The path continues on concrete, first crossing Crazylegs Lane and then immediately afterward, Breese Terrace, where you will find a map board. You are now on the actual rail bed. The trail in this section alternately cuts through or rises above the surrounding terrain and has the benefit of a lot of shade trees.

Before you continue, consider a bite to eat at Mickey's Dairy Bar, serving breakfast until 2:00 P.M., or New Orleans Take-Out, both to your left on Monroe Street. If Mediterranean/Turkish cuisine sounds more intriguing, continue up Monroe for 0.2 mile to find the Dardanelles on the left as well as a couple of coffee shops and a wine bar.

Continuing down the trail, you will pass under the Spooner Street Bridge at 1.5 miles and a rust-colored metal walking bridge at 1.7 miles. Ramps to either side will take you up to Prospect Avenue and residential neighborhoods. At this point you are below the property lines, and flower gardens line the trail to the right, while trees provide partial shade from the left.

At 1.9 miles you'll cross Edgewood Avenue; another 0.1 mile later is Commonwealth Avenue. Going left here will take you to Monroe Street,

A cyclist follows the Southwest Path in Madison under the Spooner Street Bridge.

which is 0.3 mile south. A nice collection of restaurants in that neighborhood includes Michael's Frozen Custard, Laurel Tavern, and the Tex-Mex eatery, Pasquale's.

The trail crosses Commonwealth and passes a nice wildflower garden in season before passing over a short bridge. To your right is a ramp up to Virginia Terrace, and a short path to your left exits to residential streets.

The next stretch runs higher than the houses to your left and looks out over a small ravine to your right. Beyond this is a cemetery and Glenway Golf Course. The path is straight and true until 2.9 miles where you will cross Glenway Street. On the other side find a map board, bench, and drinking water.

The shade continues on this next segment, where you are back among backyards with frequent flower gardens to the right. At 3.3 miles there is a small prairie restoration to your left, and then you cross Odana Road. There is a picnic table here in the shade. There are exits to neighborhoods at Council Crest and Parman Terrace at 3.5 miles, and then the trail crosses busy Midvale Boulevard at 3.8 miles. A stone sundial and a couple of bison statues are to your right.

The residences are set back from the trail here, and the surroundings soon become simply woods and brush. The trail is exposed from this point to the end. As you round the bend to the left, Odana Hills Golf Course is to your right. At 4.3 miles a spur trail breaks left to Hammersley Road on the north side of the Beltline (U.S. Highway 12/14). A bridge carries you over the heavy traffic, and you'll curve down a ramp to drinking water and a bench. Continue following the turn as it passes back beneath the bridge and leaves you at the southern half of Hammersley Road at 4.6 miles.

From here it is a straight shot behind Home Depot and Cub Foods along a narrow corridor between large stores and warehouses. You can slip off the trail at Cub Foods to get refreshments at 4.8 miles. Just past the supermarket you cross Verona Frontage Road and pass under US 151/Verona Road at 5.1 miles. A spur trail up to the right takes you to the head of Raymond Road, and another goes left into the Allied Drive neighborhood, which doesn't enjoy a nice reputation. Stay straight.

At 5.5 miles the path descends slightly to the right of the former rail bed. What you see going straight before you and over a bridge is the future connection to the Badger State Trail, which will be paved for the first 7 miles to where the trail is already open near Paoli. At the bottom of the sloping trail to the right is the end of the Southwest Path where it intersects with the Capital City State Trail. Going left here will require a state trail pass. You can get one at a self-pay station by following the Capital City Trail to its trailhead 0.3 mile to the right.

22 SUGAR RIVER STATE TRAIL

New Glarus is a wonderfully hospitable town with a strong Swiss heritage. Marsh and dairy farm scenery and pleasant trail towns are found along the trail.

Activities:

Location: New Glarus to Brodhead

Length: 23.1 miles, including 1.0 mile of on-street route into downtown Brodhead

Surface: The first 0.3 mile south from New Glarus is asphalt; the rest is crushed limestone with wood-planked bridges. A 1.7-mile asphalt spur trail runs south along Wisconsin Highway 69 to New Glarus Woods State Park.

Wheelchair access: Yes

Precautions: Highway crossings are at grade level. The trail is mostly open, with occasional shaded stretches. The use of sunblock is advised. Wisconsin State Trails have a carry-in/carry-out policy. Make provisions for carrying out any refuse. No trash receptacles are provided on-trail. The Wisconsin State Trail Pass is required for bicyclists age sixteen and older ($4.00 daily or $20.00 annually). The trail pass also covers usage such as cross-country skiing, horseback riding, and bicycling on state mountain bike trails and other rail trails. Passes can be purchased at the New Glarus Depot, New Glarus Woods State Park, at many local businesses and at self-pay stations at trail access parking lots. In winter you must have a Wisconsin snowmobile registration or nonresident trail use sticker.

Food and facilities: There are several restaurants in New Glarus. There are cafes in Monticello, Albany, and Brodhead, all in downtown areas away from the trail. All trail towns have taverns. Swimming pools and playgrounds are in New Glarus, Monticello, and Brodhead. Water and flush toilets are at the New Glarus Depot, Albany trail parking lot, and in Brodhead at the downtown trailhead parking lot. The Monticello trail parking lot has pit toilets.

Seasons: Open year-round

Access and parking: To start at the north end, turn west off of WI 69 onto Wisconsin Highway 39 (Sixth Avenue) in New Glarus and make an immediate right onto Railroad Street and into the New Glarus Depot trailhead parking lot. At the south end in Brodhead, park at Exchange Street and West Third Street, 2 blocks west of Wisconsin Highway 11 (Center Avenue).

Rentals: New Glarus Depot, (608) 527–2334. Earth Rider Cycling, Brodhead, (608) 897–8300 or (866) 245–5276.

Contact: Brodhead Chamber of Commerce, (608) 897–8411. New Glarus Tourism and Chamber of Commerce, (608) 527–2095 or (800) 527–6838. Sugar River State Trail, (608) 527–2334.

||||||||||||||||||||||||||||||||||||||||||||||||||||||||||||||||||||||||||||||||||||||||

When the Swiss arrived in Wisconsin in 1845, they were taken by the beauty of the green, rolling land along the Little Sugar River Valley. It had much of the character of their home in Kanton Glarus and seemed an ideal place to settle. Today the town of New Glarus gives visitors a taste of Old World hospitality and pride. The pride is evident in the flower plantings and tidy chalet-style buildings throughout the town. You'll find the hospitality at restaurants, motels, bed-and-breakfast inns, and taverns, and in the welcome you feel from the townspeople.

The Sugar River State Trail is a major focus for local tourism in New Glarus. Winding through the broad valley of the Sugar River, the trail trip is a journey through prime southern Wisconsin dairyland. For a closer look, you can tour a cheese factory in the area.

Don't be too anxious to get on the trail if you begin your trip in New Glarus. There is so much to enjoy in town, you won't even be able to scratch the surface if you leave it all for later. The downtown is just a block uphill from the depot trailhead. On the way you'll pass Puempel's Olde Tavern, which is worth a stop for a look at the 1913 murals of Swiss patriotic scenes.

Swiss fare is on all the menus in New Glarus, and the bakery is not to be missed. Several museums showcase local history and culture. The town hosts the Heidi Festival on the last full weekend in June, and the Wilhelm Tell Festival on Labor Day weekend. If all of this isn't enough, you can take a self-guided tour at the New Glarus Brewery, an excellent microbrewery

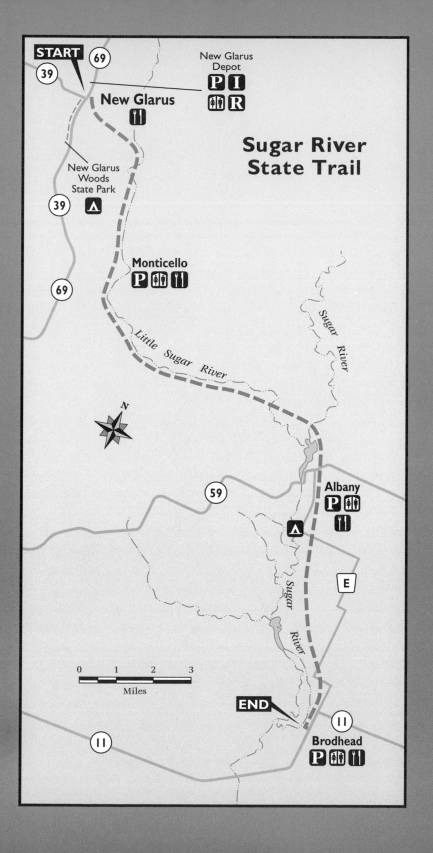

START 69 39

New Glarus Depot

P **I**

New Glarus

🚻 **R**

🍴

New Glarus Woods State Park

39

⛺

69

Monticello

P 🚻 🍴

Little Sugar River

Sugar River

Sugar River State Trail

N

59

⛺

Albany

P 🚻

🍴

Sugar River

E

0   1   2   3
Miles

END

11

Brodhead

P 🚻 🍴

11

on the east side of WI 69. You can sample whatever seasonal beer is on hand. The cherry ale is incredible, but maybe this should be left for the end of your trail trip.

Traveling south from the New Glarus Depot, the trail is asphalt paved for the first 0.3 mile until the crossing of busy WI 69. At this point an asphalt spur trail continues south on the west side of the highway for 1.7 miles to New Glarus Woods State Park.

After crossing WI 69, the Sugar River State Trail swings to the east, following the course of the Little Sugar River. As with nearly all of the trail, the close proximity to the river means that turtles are often seen. Female turtles typically return to their place of birth to lay their eggs. Box turtles and leatherbacks make their slow but determined treks across the trail. The snapping turtle looks menacing enough to make you keep your distance. Males can grow to 30 inches from tip to tail. Nobody in his right mind would go near such a monster. Females are smaller, but are just as ready to defend themselves with lightning-quick jaw snaps as their heads strike out from inside their shells.

At 3.4 miles the trail arrives at Exeter Crossing Road, part of the old wagon route from the southwest Wisconsin lead mines to Milwaukee. Another rail bed now runs parallel to the trail a short distance to the east. This is the Badger State Trail, providing a connection to Paoli to the north and Freeport, Illinois, to the south. In the future it will span the 7 miles from Paoli to Madison as well.

At 5.6 miles the two rail beds cross just north of Monticello. At 6.2 miles you arrive at a refurbished old railroad building with restrooms and shelter. Signs show an on-street bike route on East Lake Avenue that goes 0.9 mile west to Main Street, where the town's services are, and to Montesian Community Park with its playground and swimming pool. For an interesting side trip, you can go 3.5 miles west of Monticello on County Road C to the junction of County Road N. Here you can tour the Prima Kase Cheese Factory and see giant wheels of Swiss cheese being made.

From Monticello the trail swings to the east and enters its most wild and sheltered section. Along the way to Albany there are five stream crossings. The first three are small tributaries, then comes the Little Sugar River. At 14.0 miles the trail crosses the Sugar River on a long, curving bridge with a great view.

A welcome water fountain at Monticello.

At 15.9 miles the trail is in Albany at the trail parking lot and facilities. Bicycle route signs on Fourth Street show the 0.4-mile route to downtown services. South of town, at 18.4 miles, the trail crosses Atkinson Road just east of its junction with County Road E. This is where trail users would exit the rail bed to follow County Road E 0.3 mile south to the privately run Minnehaha Campground.

Nearing Brodhead, at 21.4 miles, the trail crosses Norwegian Creek on a unique covered bridge, a reconstruction of a bridge that once existed in the area. At 22.1 miles the rail bed portion of the trail ends at Decatur Road on the north edge of Brodhead. From here the route continues south on West Third Street to the downtown trailhead. Along the way you'll pass the Putnam Park swimming pool and playground. At 23.1 miles, at West Third and Exchange Streets, you arrive at the trailhead parking lot. You are just 1 block west of the Depot Museum, which highlights the history of the trail's railroad days when it was part of the Milwaukee Road.

23 TOMORROW RIVER STATE TRAIL

The trail passes through farmland and stops off in Amherst Junction, Amherst and Scandinavia for a bit of small town America. But the centerpiece is the river itself and its abundant wildlife at the center of the trail.

Activities:

Note: There is no special grooming for skiing.

Location: Plover to Scandinavia

Length: 18.7 miles (plus 1.8 miles of on-road trail between the two segments)

Surface: Crushed limestone

Wheelchair access: Yes

Precautions: There are frequent road crossings throughout the trail. In Amherst the on-road segment follows 0.5 mile on a country road and crosses Old Highway 10. The on-road portion is rather hilly. Horses have a separate parallel trail and should never be on the limestone trail except in posted areas where the two are shared. Dogs must be leashed at all times. The trail is mostly open, with occasional shaded stretches. The use of sunblock is advised. Wisconsin State Trails have a carry-in/carry-out policy. Make provisions for carrying out any refuse. No trash receptacles are provided on-trail. The Wisconsin State Trail Pass is required for bicyclists age sixteen and older ($4.00 daily or $20.00 annually). The trail pass also covers usage such as cross-country skiing, horseback riding, and bicycling on state mountain bike trails and other rail trails. Passes can be purchased at the Portage County and Waupaca County Parks offices and at self-pay stations at the Plover and Amherst trail parking lots.

Food and facilities: Plover offers a variety of shops and restaurants west of the trailhead. Arnott has a bar and a couple of cafes, and there's a tavern just off the trail on Smokey Road in the tiny town of Fancher. Amherst Junction has several local eateries as does Amherst, though the latter is 0.8 mile south of the trail. Pit toilets are located just off the trail near Lake Emily Park, and within the park are more extensive facilities. The trailhead in Scandinavia is just south of the downtown area, where you will find more places for refreshments and restrooms.

Seasons: Open year-round

Access and parking: The Plover trailhead is located just north of County Road B on Twin Towers Road, 2 miles east of the Interstate 39/County Road B interchange. The trailhead on Custer Road is 0.7 mile north of County Road B. Custer Road is 7 miles east of the I–39/County Road B interchange. The trailhead at Amherst Junction is on Second Street south of the intersection of Old Highway 10 and Wisconsin Highway 161. Cate Park, north of Amherst on County Road A, has parking and a short spur trail to the state trail. Scandinavia's trail access is south of the bridge over Wisconsin Highway 49/Main Street on the south edge of town. Additional parking and public restrooms are available at Lake Emily Park.

Rentals: Nature Treks, Stevens Point, offers free shuttle service within Portage County; (715) 254–0247, www.naturetrekrentals.net.

Contact: Portage County Parks Department, Stevens Point, (715) 346–1433, www.co.portage.wi.us. Waupaca County Parks Department, Waupaca, (715) 258–6243.

||||||||||||||||||||||||||||||||||||||||||||||||||||||||||||||||||||||||||||||||||||

*W*aupaca is a Native American word that means "tomorrow." The Tomorrow River is actually a branch of the Waupaca River, so in a sense they share the name. It was a good trout stream before the mill was constructed in Amherst and created a millpond. But a new day has risen on the river, and through the hard work of dam removal and restoration, the trout are biting once again. The river passes under the trail about halfway, and this is surely the nicest place to stop and take in the view.

The rest of the trail passes through a mix of forest and agricultural fields, all set on what was a massive glacial lake and outwash plain in central Wisconsin around 10,000 years ago. During dry periods you can see the dust blow off the fields. The sandy soil was considered useless, but

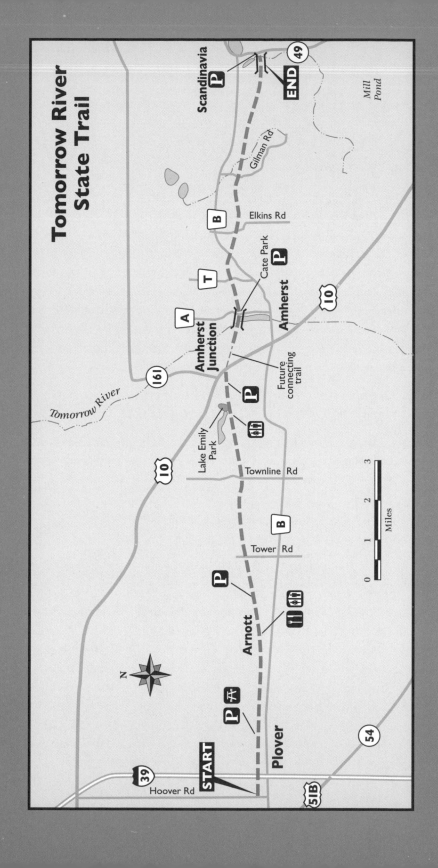

today irrigation makes the land green with crops, including corn, green beans, and soybeans. The soil is especially good for potatoes. Excess moisture drains through to prevent rotting, and it is rare that a heavy rain ever delays a harvest.

The trailhead is in Plover and departs at the southern end of the 25-mile Green Circle Trail. Initially the trail runs alongside the north side of the railroad tracks. Head east along the diminutive Lake Clar-Re to your left and pass warehouses and the backs of businesses to your right just before you go under I–39. The underside of the overpass is lined with swallow nests. The section beyond here can be closed temporarily for aerial spraying in growing season.

At 1.5 miles you will come to the Twin Towers Drive parking lot, which may be a better starting point for those with vehicles. Here you'll find picnic tables, a map board, and a self-pay tube for the trail fee.

At 2.0 miles the trail takes over the rail bed and begins crossing farmland on what is basically a land bridge overlooking irrigated fields to either side. The trail cuts through low-rising hills at about 3.0 miles, so that it becomes a sort of corridor with scattered boulders. This doesn't last long, and soon the trail becomes even with the terrain. You'll see the orderly rows of tall planted pines in the wooded stretches, and a trailside sign tells the story of the glacial formation of the land.

At 4.0 miles you can stop for drinks at Arnott, which has an organic café, a bakery, and an egg roll factory. Past the town you can see amber waves of grain undulating in summer breezes. Another sight is the irrigation operation. A few diesel-powered pumps are located close to the trail, and you can see the results casting rainbows over the fields of beans and potatoes.

At 5.1 miles you will cross Custer Road, where there is another parking area for the trail. The trail starts to bend left slightly, and more boulders left behind by the glaciers poke up out of the underbrush to the right. The horse trail sometimes shares the bike path, but here it descends to the level of the fields.

At 6.1 miles cross Tower Road, and another mile later you will reach Smokey Spur Road. The Smokey Spur Bar to your right sports a faded Hamm's sign and neon Point Beer logo. The trail goes gently downhill from here, crossing County Road K at 7.6 miles. The terrain varies between farm

A beautiful view overlooking the Tomorrow River.

fields and forest with oak trees. You'll cross Townline Road after another 0.5 mile as the trail bends farther north a bit more. At 9.7 miles cross Edgewater Drive and then look for a sign for the pit toilets 0.1 mile later on the left. This is part of the 143-acre Lake Emily Park, where you will find camping, showers, a playground, drinking water, swimming, fishing, boating, picnic tables, and hiking trails. To get to the park, go left at Lake Drive at 10.0 miles. The park is open May 1 through October 31.

You are now entering Amherst Junction. The railroad was designed with an underpass for one of the two sets of tracks that meet at this junction. It was intended to avoid hazards. The trail takes you into town at 10.8 miles. Crossing the Second Street bridge, you will find a gravel and grass parking lot on your left, along with picnic tables, a map board, and a self-pay tube.

Plans are in the works to develop the 1-mile stretch of empty rail bed that lies between here and where the trail picks up again at Alm Road to the east of town. The primary concern is building a bridge over Old Highway 10 (which you need to cross anyway on the on-road segment).

From where the trail end, proceed left 0.5 mile on Second Street, which becomes WI 161 after it crosses Old Highway 10. Go to Lake Meyers Road and turn right, going 0.7 mile to Alm Road, then turn (right) south for another 0.7-mile stretch before picking up the trail again. The Lake Meyers Road segment offers some steep hills, which may be a shock after the ease of the rail bed.

Ride another 0.5 mile from Alm Road to reach the bridge over the Tomorrow River at 13.2 miles. The bridge offers nice views of the water and the Amherst Mill Pond. This is a good place to spot waterfowl and listen for bullfrogs. Just past the bridge on the right, a spur trail leads to Cate Park in Amherst, with parking and a picnic area only. You can ride into Amherst along the road there, but it is another 0.8 mile. Remember there are no facilities along this segment after Amherst.

From the bridge begins the loveliest portion of the trail. Cross County Road A at 13.3 miles as you enter into abundant forest. At 14.0 miles pass Turtle Lake down off the steep edge of the rail bed to the left. In the spring and summer, you'll see myriad prairie flowers alongside the trail. You'll reach County Road T at 14.2 miles; another 0.8 mile puts you at County Road B. At 15.5 miles cross Elkins Road, and in the middle of the forest at 16.3 miles, cross the county line from Portage into Waupaca. A boulder there stands as a memorial to trail promoter Greg Marr. This portion of the trail offers about all the shade you are going to get, and it is patchy at best. Raspberries are a nice reward for coming this far in midsummer.

Cross Gilman Road, and then at 17.4 miles you can see Peterson Creek flowing under the rail bed through a culvert. The trail opens up again here as it passes through open fields, and on a hot summer day this will be merciless if you've done the whole trail and haven't brought enough water. You will cross Gurholt Road at 19.3 miles as you enter into Scandinavia. Trees and brush will begin to close in on the trail once again as it bends left. Cross the bridge over Main Street at 20.3 miles and follow a long ramp down to the right to the small parking lot on the east side of WI 49 (Main Street).

The rail bed continues from the bridge, but plans are to develop the trail another 11 miles to Manawa.

24 WILD GOOSE STATE TRAIL

This quiet trail that skirts the west side of the vast Horicon National Wildlife Refuge is a haven for songbirds. There are pleasant parks in Juneau and Oakfield.

Activities:

Note: Horseback riding is permitted on an adjacent path on the southernmost 7.5 miles. ATV use is permitted from December 31 through March 31 in Dodge County only.

Location: Fond du Luc to Clyman Junction

Length: 33.7 miles

Surface: Crushed limestone with wood-planked bridges, several short on-road paved sections

Wheelchair access: Yes

Precautions: There are on-street sections in Burnett and Juneau. Numerous crossings, some of busy highways, require caution. There are very few services available between Oakfield and Juneau. Many sections of the trail are open, with occasional shaded stretches. The use of sunblock is advised. Take care not to frighten horses on the adjacent riding path. Wisconsin State Trails have a carry-in/carry-out policy. Make provisions for carrying out any refuse. No trash receptacles are provided on-trail. Despite the fact that it is a Wisconsin State Trail, no fee is required, but donations are recommended. In winter you must have a Wisconsin snowmobile registration or nonresident trail use sticker.

Food and facilities: There are no facilities at the northern trailhead. Numerous fast-food and fine dining establishments are found nearby along U.S. Highway 151 in Fond du Lac. Trail riders may use restrooms at the Rolling Meadows Clubhouse 0.3 mile northwest of the trailhead on Rolling Meadows Road. Oakfield has a grocery store, and its Town Park has a shelter, playground, water, and flush toilets. There are restrooms at the Marsh Haven Nature Center. There is a tavern near the trail route in Burnett and a playground and water at Fireman's Park a few blocks west of the trail across

Wisconsin Highway 26. A convenience store and porta-type toilets are located at the Wisconsin Highway 33 trail crossing. Juneau has a restaurant, grocery, and City Park with a shelter, playground, water, and flush toilets. There is a porta-type toilet at the southern trailhead at Clyman Junction.

Seasons: Open year-round

Access and parking: For the northern trailhead, from US 151 southwest of Fond du Lac, turn southeast on Rolling Meadows Road and travel 0.7 mile to the trailhead. For the southern trailhead, from WI 26, turn east on Wisconsin Highway 60 and travel 1.2 miles to the trailhead. More comfortable trailheads are located in Oakfield and Juneau. From US 151, take County Road Y 3.3 miles south to County Road D in Oakfield, turn east on County Road D, and travel 0.1 mile to the Town Park. From WI 26 in Juneau, turn east on East Grove Street (Wisconsin Highway 115), travel 0.1 mile, and turn right (south) on South Fair Street. Travel 1 block to Lincoln Drive and cross it into the City Park parking lot.

Rentals: Fond du Lac Cyclery, (920) 923–3211

Contact: Fond du Lac Convention and Visitors Bureau, (800) 937–9123 or (920) 923–3010, www.fdl.com. Wisconsin Department of Natural Resources, (608) 266–2181. Dodge County Land Resources and Parks, (920) 386–3700.

|||||||||||||||||||||||||||||||||||||||||||||||||||||||||||||||||||||||||||||||||||

Nature reigns along the Wild Goose State Trail. The vast Horicon Marsh is a magnet for migrating waterfowl. In the fall thousands upon thousands of Canada geese pass through, their chevron-shaped formations pointed south. In summer the trail is alive with songbirds seeking the brushy trailside shelter.

The appealing small towns of Oakfield and Juneau invite trail users with their pleasant town parks. The city of Fond du Lac has all the services you might imagine, plus other attractions: At picturesque Lakeside Park on Lake Winnebago, you can visit a lighthouse; Historic Galloway House and Village showcases a stately Victorian mansion and twenty-three period buildings depicting nineteenth-century lifestyles.

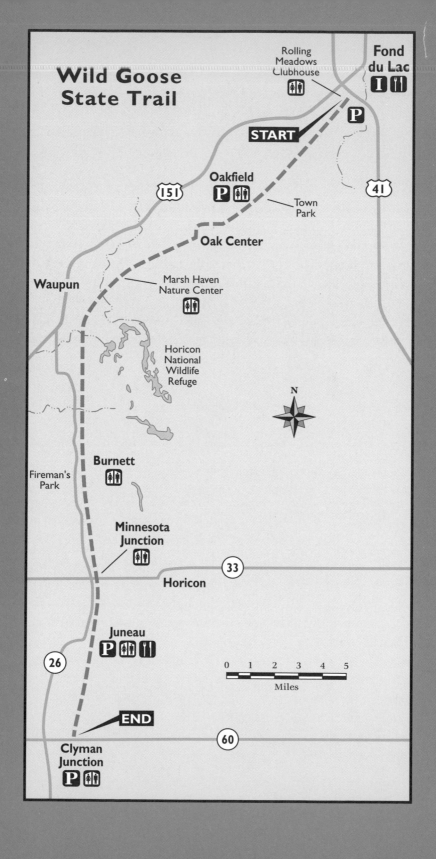

Trailside brush is a haven for songbirds along the Wild Goose State Trail.

Traveling southeast from the northern trailhead near Fond du Lac, the trail is isolated from farm fields by trees and brushy growth along the railroad grade. At 5.7 miles the trail crosses County Road D in Oakfield. Pleasant Town Park is located 1 block east on County Road D.

Between 10.5 and 12.0 miles you can get a glimpse of the vast expanse of Horicon Marsh through occasional breaks in the trailside brush to the south. At 13.3 miles, just before the Wisconsin Highway 49 crossing, look for a small sign for a picnic area on the southeast side of the trail. A little path leads you off the trail to the Marsh Haven Nature Center. A privately run center and wildlife art gallery, Marsh Haven features the natural and cultural history of the marsh, and you can get a great view from the observation tower.

Leaving Marsh Haven Nature Center, you begin an 8.6-mile stretch without any services. This is a nice stretch of trail, though, with lots of shade and warbling songbirds. At 20.1 miles look for the tall brick Gothic steeple of Immanuel Kirche church to the west of the trail. At 22.3 miles you reach the little village of Burnett, where the trail takes a short on-street detour to the west. Turn right (west) off of the trail onto Depot Street and travel

Horicon Marsh,
A Tribute to the Conservation Movement

If you look across the vast 32,000-acre Horicon Marsh—where the wind can make the reeds ripple like waves on the ocean, and waterfowl glide in by the thousands to land in the open-water areas—it is hard to imagine that anything has changed since time immemorial. What you see today is certainly similar to what the native Ho Chunk (Winnebago) culture looked upon, but it has not always been so.

The Ho Chunk prized the marsh. It not only sustained them, but was a spiritual place as well. Recent discoveries on the eastern high ground that borders the marsh show celestial alignments of ancient stones and mounds with solstice sunsets.

When European settlers arrived, they viewed the marsh as a wasteland. First, in 1846 a dam was built that turned the marsh into what was claimed to be "the largest man-made lake in the world." Legal action forced the removal of the dam after twenty-three years. Horicon returned to marshland and a wildlife haven, but late in the nineteenth century, market hunters came and took the waterfowl in such great numbers that the prices in Milwaukee fell to 10 cents a bird. Then a number of canals were built to drain the marsh for farming.

Despite the decimation, Horicon couldn't be tamed for successful agriculture. In the late 1920s conservationists persuaded federal and state governments to purchase the land. Horicon National Wildlife Refuge was created on the northern 21,000 acres, and the state Horicon Marsh Wildlife Area on the southern 11,000 acres. The restored marsh ultimately grew to nearly 50 square miles. In 1942 only about 450 geese visited; today 70,000 is typical, and the number has at times been estimated as twice that many.

> The history of the marsh and information on the 250-plus species of birds it attracts can be explored at the Horicon National Wildlife Refuge Visitor Center on the east side of the marsh on County Road Z, 8 miles north of Mayville. You can get up close in a canoe or on a boat tour at Blue Heron Landing at the Sinnissippi River bridge in Horicon, 3 miles east of the Wild Goose State Trail on WI 33.

about 30 yards to an unnamed street. Turn left (south) on the unnamed street, travel 0.2 mile to Maple Street, and turn left (east) on a path that returns you to the off-road trail. You'll be ready for a rest after the long trail stretch, so follow Depot Street west 0.2 mile to WI 26 and cross the highway to Fireman's Park.

Continuing south, at 26.5 miles you come to the busy WI 33 crossing at Minnesota Junction. There is a convenience store at this intersection. At 29.0 miles you reach East Center Street in Juneau. At this point you need to take a short on-street detour to continue following the trail to the south. Turn left (west) on East Center Street, travel about 40 yards, then turn left (south) on South Depot Street. Travel 2 blocks to East Oak Grove Street, turn left (east), travel about 40 yards to the off-road trail at 29.3 miles, and turn right (south).

While you are in Juneau, you may want to take a break by visiting the town businesses on East Oak Street (halfway between East Center Street and East Oak Grove Street) or shaded City Park. To reach the park, take East Oak Grove Street 2 blocks west to South Fair Street, turn left (south), and travel 1 block to Lincoln Drive and the park entrance.

Heading south from Juneau, you begin traveling through Dodge County's famous drumlin fields. You are moving in the same direction the great continental glacier did when it carved out Lake Winnebago and Horicon Marsh and created this vast area of elongated, parallel hills. At 33.7 miles you reach the southern trailhead at WI 60 at Clyman Junction. You won't find anything here because the town disappeared with the railroad.

More Rail Trails

In a number of places around the state are rail trails that for one reason or another don't measure up to the criteria for "Wisconsin's Top Rail Trails." It's not that they aren't pleasant places to spend some time; we simply needed to make some decisions because of space limitations. All of the following trails are passable to some extent, though their level of day-to-day maintenance may be suspect. Future editions of this book may upgrade some of these trails to "Top" status if more segments are completed, they become safer to use, or they're connected to other trails. For now, consider these trails a little more of an adventure than the others and use them accordingly.

25 BANNERMAN TRAIL

Activities:

Location: Redgranite to 5 miles south of Wautoma

Length: 7 miles

Surface: Dirt

Contact: Waushara County Parks, Wautoma, WI 54982; (920) 787–7037. Village of Redgranite, P.O. Box 500, Redgranite, WI 54970; (920) 566–2381.

26 BUFFALO RIVER STATE PARK TRAIL

Activities:

Location: Fairchild to Mondovi

Length: 36.4 miles

Surface: Gravel, ballast, dirt, limestone

Contact: Perrott State Park, W26247 Sullivan Road, P.O. Box 407, Trempealeau, WI 54661; (608) 534–6409

 CATTAIL TRAIL

Activities:

Location: Almena to Amery

Length: 17.8 miles

Surface: Gravel, ballast, dirt

Contact: Polk County Information Center, 710 Highway 35 South, St. Croix Falls, WI 54024; (715) 483–1410, www.polkcountytourism.com

28 CHEESE COUNTRY RECREATION TRAIL

Activities:

Location: Mineral Point to Monroe

Length: 47 miles

Surface: Crushed limestone with concrete bridges

Contact: Tri-County Trail Commission, 627 Washington Street, Darlington, WI 53530; (608) 776–5706 or (608) 574–2911, www.tricountytrails.com

29 CLEAR LAKE–CLAYTON TRAIL

Activities:

Location: Clear Lake to Clayton

Length: 11 miles

Surface: Ballast

Contact: Polk County Information Center, 710 Highway 35 South, St. Croix Falls, WI 54024; (715) 483–1410, www.polkcountytourism.com

30 DEVIL'S RIVER STATE TRAIL (IN DEVELOPMENT)

Activities:

Location: Denmark to Rockwood

Length: 14 miles

Surface: Crushed limestone

Contact: Wisconsin Department of Natural Resources, (608) 266–2621

31 EISENBAHN STATE TRAIL

Activities:

Location: West Bend to Fond du Lac County

Length: 25 miles

Surface: Crushed limestone, asphalt in West Bend

Contact: Washington County Parks, 333 East Washington Street, West Bend, WI 53095; (262) 335–4445. Fond du Lac County Parks, 160 South Macy Street, Fond Du Lac, WI 54935; (920) 929–3135.

32 FOX RIVER STATE RECREATIONAL TRAIL

Activities:

Location: Green Bay to Brown-Calumet County line

Length: 19.5 miles

Surface: Asphalt, crushed limestone

Contact: Brown County Facility and Park Management Office, 325 East Walnut Street, Room 220, Green Bay, WI 54301; (920) 448-4466

33 HANK AARON STATE TRAIL

Activities:

Location: Lake Michigan shoreline to Miller Park, Milwaukee (to be extended to Waukesha County line by 2009)

Length: 7 miles (plus a 5.5-mile extension on a rail bed by 2009)

Surface: Asphalt, some on-road segments

Contact: Greater Milwaukee Convention and Visitors Bureau, (800) 231–0903. Trail Manager, Wisconsin Department of Natural Resources, (414) 263–8559.

34 HIAWATHA TRAIL (BEARSKIN-HIAWATHA STATE TRAIL)

Activities:

Location: Sara Park, Tomahawk

Length: 6.6 miles

Surface: Crushed red granite with wood-planked bridges

Contact: Lincoln County Forestry Land and Parks, 1106 East Eighth Street, Merrill, WI 54452-1100; (715) 536–0327

35 HILLSBORO TRAIL

Activities:

Location: Hillsboro to "400" State Trail at Union Center

Length: 4.3 miles

Surface: Crushed limestone with wood-planked bridges

Contact: Hillsboro City Hall, P.O. Box 447, Hillsboro, WI 54634; (608) 489–2521, www.hillsborowi.com

36 KIMBALL CREEK TRAIL

Activities:

Location: Nicolet National Forest

Length: 13.6 miles

Surface: Ballast, dirt

Contact: Chequamegon-Nicolet National Forest, Eagle River Ranger District, 1247 East Wall Street, Eagle River, WI 54521; (715) 479–2827

37 LAKE COUNTRY RECREATION TRAIL

Activities:

Location: Delafield to Waukesha

Length: 9.5 miles

Surface: Asphalt, crushed limestone

Contact: Waukesha County Department of Parks and Land Use, 1320 Pewaukee Road, Room 230, Waukesha, WI 53188–3868; (262) 548–7790. Get an online map at www.waukeshacounty.gov/parks/biking.

38 LINCOLN COUNTY SNOWMOBILE TRAIL

Activities:

Location: Tomahawk to Lincoln-Oneida County line

Length: 15 miles

Surface: Gravel, ballast

Contact: Lincoln County Forestry Land and Parks, 1106 East Eighth Street, Merrill, WI 54452-1100; (715) 536–0327

39 MASCOUTIN VALLEY STATE TRAIL

Activities:

Location: Berlin to Ripon/ Rosendale to Fond du Lac

Length: 10.3 miles/9 miles

Surface: Crushed limestone

Contact: Winnebago County Parks Department, 500 East County Road Y, Oshkosh, WI 54901-9774; (920) 424–0042. Fond du Lac County Parks, 160 South Macy Street, Fond du Lac, WI 54935; (920) 929–3135.

40 MOUNTAIN–BAY STATE TRAIL (DELLY TRAIL)

Activities:

Location: Duck Creek (near Green Bay) to Kelly (near Wausau)

Length: 83.4 miles

Surface: Crushed limestone with wood-planked bridges

Contact: Marathon County Parks, 212 River Drive, Wausau, WI 54403; (715) 261–1550. Shawano County Parks Department, 311 North Main Street, Shawano, WI 54166; (715) 526–6766. Brown County Park Department, 305 East Walnut Street #304, Green Bay, WI 54301; (920) 448–4466, www .mountain-baytrail.org.

41 MRK TRAIL

Activities:
Note: Dogs must be kept on a leash.

Location: Racine to Caledonia

Length: 4 miles with plans to extend to the Milwaukee County line

Surface: Crushed stone, gravel, ballast

Contact: Racine County Public Works Department,14200 Washington Avenue, Sturtevant, WI 53177-1253; (262) 886–8440

42 NEW BERLIN TRAIL

Activities:

Location: Waukesha to West Allis

Length: 7 miles

Surface: Asphalt

Contact: Waukesha County Department of Parks and Land Use,1320 Pewaukee Road, Room 230, Waukesha, WI 53188-3868; (262) 548–7790

43 NEW LONDON TO SEYMOUR STATE TRAIL (UNDER CONSTRUCTION)

Location: New London to Seymour in Outagamie County

Length: 23 miles

Surface: Crushed limestone

Contact: Outagamie County Parks, 1375 East Broadway Drive, Appleton, WI 54915; (920) 832–4790

44 NORTH SHORE TRAIL

Activities:

Note: Dogs must be kept on a leash.

Location: Racine to Kenosha County line

Length: 3 miles

Surface: Crushed stone, gravel

Seasons: Open year-round

Contact: Racine County Public Works Department,14200 Washington Avenue, Sturtevant, WI 53177-1253; (262) 886–8440

45 OLIVER–WRENSHALL TRAIL

Activities:

Location: Oliver to Wrenshall, Minnesota

Length: 12 miles

Surface: Dirt

Contact: Douglas County Forestry Department, P.O. Box 211, Solon Springs, WI 54873-0211; (715) 378–2219

46 PECATONICA STATE PARK TRAIL

Activities:

Location: Calamine to Belmont

Length: 13.5 miles

Surface: Crushed stone with concrete bridges

Contact: Tri-County Trail Commission, 627 Washington Street, Darlington, WI 53530; (608) 776–5706, www.tricountytrails.com

47 PELISHEK NATURE TRAIL

Activities:

Location: Clinton to Darien

Length: 7 miles

Surface: Gravel, ballast

Contact: County of Rock Park and Conservation Division, 3715 Newville Road, Janesville, WI 53545-8844; (608) 757–5450

48 PINE LINE RECREATION TRAIL

Activities:

Location: Medford to Prentice

Length: 26.2 miles

Surface: Crushed stone, gravel

Contact: Price County Tourism Office,126 Cherry Street, Phillips, WI 54555-1249; (800) 269–4505

49 PINE RIVER TRAIL

Activities:

Location: Lone Rock to Richland Center

Length: 15 miles

Surface: Crushed limestone with wood-planked bridges

Contact: Richland Center Chamber of Commerce, 397 West Seminary Street, P.O. Box 128, Richland Center, WI 53581; (608) 647–6205

50 RILEY LAKE SNOWMOBILE TRAIL

Activities: 🚶 🏇 🛷 🌙 🎣

Location: Chequamegon-Nicolet National Forest

Length: 23 miles

Surface: Dirt

Contact: Chequamegon-Nicolet National Forest, 1170 Fourth Avenue South, Park Falls, WI 54552-1921; (715) 762–2461

51 ROCK RIVER PARKWAY TRAIL

Activities: 🚶 🚴 ⛸ 🐟 🐕 🚴

Location: Janesville to Beloit

Length: 5.1 miles

Surface: Asphalt, crushed stone, grass, concrete

Contact: Janesville Leisure Services, 18 North Jackson Street, Janesville, WI 53545; (608) 755–3025

52 SAUNDERS GRADE RECREATION TRAIL

Activities: 🚶 🏇 🛷 ⛷ 🌙

Location: Solon Springs to Lake Superior

Length: 8.4 miles

Surface: Ballast, cinders

Contact: Douglas County Forestry Department, P.O. Box 211, Solon Springs, WI 54873-0211; (715) 378–2219

53 SEVEN WATERS TRAIL

Activities:

Note: Dogs must be kept on a leash.

Location: Burlington to Waukesha County line

Length: 15.5 miles

Surface: Crushed limestone, some asphalt

Contact: Racine County Public Works Department, 14200 Washington Avenue, Sturtevant, WI 53177-1253; (262) 886–8440

54 TRI-COUNTY CORRIDOR TRAIL

Activities:

Location: Ashland to Superior

Length: 61.8 miles

Surface: Crushed stone, ballast

Contact: Bayfield County Tourism, P.O. Box 832, Washburn, WI 54891; (800) 472–6338

55 TUSCOBIA STATE TRAIL

Activities:

Location: Park Falls to Rice Lake

Length: 74 miles

Surface: Gravel, ballast

Contact: Price County Tourism Department, 126 Cherry Street, Phillips, WI 54555; (800) 269–4505, www.tuscobiatrail.com

56 WILD RIVERS STATE TRAIL

Activities:

Location: Rice Lake to just south of Superior

Length: 90 miles

Surface: Ballast, cinders

Contact: Douglas County Forestry Department, P.O. Box 211, Solon Springs, WI 54873; (715) 378–2219

57 WILDWOOD TRAIL

Activities:

Location: Woodville to St. Croix County line

Length: 7.6 miles

Surface: Crushed limestone

Contact: Parks Department St. Croix County, 1049 Rustic Road Three, Glenwood City, WI 54013; (715) 265–4613

58 WIOUWASH TRAIL–NORTH

Activities:

Location: Aniwa to New London

Length: 20 miles

Surface: Crushed limestone with wood-planked bridges

Contact: Winnebago County Parks, 500 East Sunnyview Road, County Road Y, Oshkosh, WI 54901; (920) 424–0042. Outagamie County Parks, 1375 East Broadway Drive, Appleton, WI 54915; (920) 832–4790. Shawano County Parks, 311 North Main Street, Shawano, WI 54166; (715) 526–6766.

59 WIOUWASH TRAIL–SOUTH

Activities:

Location: Hortonville to Oshkosh

Length: 20.3 miles

Surface: Crushed limestone with wood-planked bridges

Contact: Outagamie County Parks, 1375 East Broadway Drive, Appleton, WI 54915; (920) 832–4790

ABOUT THE AUTHOR

Phil Van Valkenberg has been bicycling in Wisconsin since he got a Chinese red Schwinn Spitfire for his tenth birthday in 1955. Even earlier, he was drawing maps and exploring the fascinating world along railroad grades. He remembers fondly when at age six he and a friend asked a steam locomotive engineer if they could have a ride. The engineer reached down to help them up the ladder. For a brief few minutes they rode in the fascinating cab, a world of valves, pipes, and gauges, as the engine chugged to the roundhouse. As an adult, both pedaling and railroad interests coalesced when he began writing about bicycle touring, and the state of Wisconsin started converting abandoned railroad grades into pedestrian/bicycle trails. He has authored eight books about trails and routes in Wisconsin and the Midwest for bicyclists, cross-country skiers, and snowshoers. Today he lives near the Chequamegon National Forest in Cable, Wisconsin.

ABOUT THE EDITOR

Kevin Revolinski inherited a love of the outdoors from his father and can remember biking the dirt trails alongside the railroad tracks near where he grew up in Marshfield, Wisconsin. He is the author of *60 Hikes within 60 Miles of Madison, The Wisconsin Beer Guide: A Travel Companion,* and is co-author of *Best in Tent Camping: Wisconsin.* His articles and photography have appeared in a variety of publications, including the *Chicago Tribune, Wisconsin State Journal,* and Madison's *Isthmus.*